KNOWING THE BIBLE

J. I. Packer, Theological Editor
Dane C. Ortlund, Series Editor
Lane T. Dennis, Executive Editor

• • • • • •

Genesis	Psalms	Jonah, Micah, and Nahum	Ephesians
Exodus	Proverbs		Philippians
Leviticus	Ecclesiastes	Haggai, Zechariah, and Malachi	Colossians and Philemon
Numbers	Song of Solomon		
Deuteronomy	Isaiah	Matthew	1–2 Thessalonians
Joshua	Jeremiah	Mark	1–2 Timothy and Titus
Judges	Lamentations, Habakkuk, and Zephaniah	Luke	
Ruth and Esther		John	
1–2 Samuel	Ezekiel	Acts	Hebrews
1–2 Kings	Daniel	Romans	James
1–2 Chronicles	Hosea	1 Corinthians	1–2 Peter and Jude
Ezra and Nehemiah	Joel, Amos, and Obadiah	2 Corinthians	1–3 John
Job		Galatians	Revelation

• • • • • •

J. I. PACKER is the former Board of Governors' Professor of Theology at Regent College (Vancouver, BC). Dr. Packer earned his DPhil at the University of Oxford. He is known and loved worldwide as the author of the best-selling book *Knowing God*, as well as many other titles on theology and the Christian life. He serves as the General Editor of the ESV Bible and as the Theological Editor for the *ESV Study Bible*.

LANE T. DENNIS is CEO of Crossway, a not-for-profit publishing ministry. Dr. Dennis earned his PhD from Northwestern University. He is Chair of the ESV Bible Translation Oversight Committee and Executive Editor of the *ESV Study Bible*.

DANE C. ORTLUND is Chief Publishing Officer at Crossway. He is a graduate of Covenant Theological Seminary (MDiv, ThM) and Wheaton College (BA, PhD). Dr. Ortlund has authored several books and scholarly articles in the areas of Bible, theology, and Christian living.

HEBREWS

A 12-WEEK STUDY

Matthew Z. Capps

CROSSWAY®

WHEATON, ILLINOIS

Trade paperback ISBN: 978-1-4335-4358-6
EPub ISBN: 978-1-4335-4361-6
PDF ISBN: 978-1-4335-4359-3
Mobipocket ISBN: 978-1-4335-4360-9

Crossway is a publishing ministry of Good News Publishers.

VP		30	29	28	27	26	25	24	23	22	21	20
18	17	16	15	14	13	12	11	10	9	8	7	6

TABLE OF CONTENTS

SERIES PREFACE

KNOWING THE BIBLE, as the series title indicates, was created to help readers know and understand the meaning, the message, and the God of the Bible. Each volume in the series consists of 12 units that progressively take the reader through a clear, concise study of that book of the Bible. In this way, any given volume can fruitfully be used in a 12-week format either in group study, such as in a church-based context, or in individual study. Of course, these 12 studies could be completed in fewer or more than 12 weeks, as convenient, depending on the context in which they are used.

Each study unit gives an overview of the text at hand before digging into it with a series of questions for reflection or discussion. The unit then concludes by highlighting the gospel of grace in each passage ("Gospel Glimpses"), identifying whole-Bible themes that occur in the passage ("Whole-Bible Connections"), and pinpointing Christian doctrines that are affirmed in the passage ("Theological Soundings").

The final component to each unit is a section for reflecting on personal and practical implications from the passage at hand. The layout provides space for recording responses to the questions proposed, and we think readers need to do this to get the full benefit of the exercise. The series also includes definitions of key words. These definitions are indicated by a note number in the text and are found at the end of each chapter.

Lastly, to help understand the Bible in this deeper way, we urge readers to use the ESV Bible and the *ESV Study Bible*, which are available in various print and digital formats, including online editions at esv.org. The Knowing the Bible series is also available online.

May the Lord greatly bless your study as you seek to know him through knowing his Word.

J. I. Packer
Lane T. Dennis

WEEK 1: OVERVIEW

▲

The anonymous book of Hebrews is a unique contribution to the canon of Scripture. Hebrews begins without an introduction, like many other New Testament letters, though it closes with blessings and greetings (Heb. 13:23–24). The author sheds light on the form of Hebrews by referring to his writing as a "word of exhortation" (v. 22). Hebrews is written in a pastoral voice with many practical exhortations, leading many to consider it a single sermon or sermonic discourse, addressed to converts from Judaism under pressure to revert to Jewish faith.

Hebrews is also considered one of the most beautifully written and stylistically polished books of the New Testament, a literary masterpiece. The author is a master of rhetorical debate and persuasion. He also demonstrates his profound theological prowess with his use of imagery, metaphor, allusion, Old Testament analogy, and typology. Throughout his exposition and exhortation, the author weaves a beautiful tapestry of biblical theology with the aim of exalting the supremacy of Jesus Christ.

The central motif of Hebrews is "Jesus Christ is better" (the words "better," "more," and "greater" appear a combined 25 times). In many ways, the glory of God as revealed in Jesus Christ is the gravitational center of Hebrews. The first 12 chapters outline a powerful theological argument for the superiority of Christ above all created things and all Old Testament counterparts, with a special focus on encouraging the reader to persevere in the faith that has Christ at its center. Through encouraging words, firm warnings, and contrasting examples, the author often calls the reader to respond to Christ in worship.

Placing It in the Larger Story

Hebrews contains 35 direct quotations from the Old Testament, along with many allusions and references. With the Old Testament background in mind, the author argues that God's glory and redemptive plan are finally and most clearly revealed in Jesus Christ. The superiority of Jesus is demonstrated in that he is greater than any angel, priest, or old covenant institution. Christ is the complete atoning sacrifice and final priest. In him we see the fulfillment of all the Old Testament hopes and promises, ushering in the long-awaited new covenant age.

Key Verse

"He [Jesus] is the radiance of the glory of God and the exact imprint of his nature, and he upholds the universe by the word of his power. After making purification for sins, he sat down at the right hand of the Majesty on high . . ." (Heb. 1:3).

Date and Historical Background

Hebrews was written in the first century, probably before AD 70. The author of Hebrews does not name himself. There has been much conjecture as to his identity; as the early Christian theologian Origen (d. c. AD 245) said, "only God knows" who he is. However, we can be sure that the author was familiar with his audience, for he longed to be reunited with them (Heb. 13:19) and is able to give them news of Timothy, Paul's second-in-command (v. 23).

The traditional title "To the Hebrews" reflects the ancient notion that the original audience was primarily made up of Jewish Christians. One can safely assume that the audience was familiar with, and well understood, the many quotations and allusions to the Old Testament. Certainly, the author was addressing professing Christians with this letter; several times the author urges them to maintain their confession and faith (3:6, 14; 4:14; 10:23).

Outline

     D. Warning five: against refusing the speaker (12:25–29)

  X. Final Exhortations (13:1–25)

     A. Sacrifices pleasing to God (13:1–19)

     B. Benediction (13:20–21)

     C. Final greetings (13:22–25)

▶ As You Get Started

What is your present understanding of how Hebrews helps us to grasp the whole storyline of the Bible? Do you have an idea as to how aspects of the Old Testament are shown to be fulfilled in Hebrews?

What is your current understanding of what Hebrews contributes to Christian theology? How does this book clarify our understanding of the major doctrines of the Christian faith?

Is there any Old Testament imagery in Hebrews that is particularly confusing to you? Are there any specific questions that you hope to have answered through this study?

Week 2: Introduction: The Supremacy of Jesus Christ

Hebrews 1:1–4

The Place of the Passage

The opening verses of Hebrews present Jesus as the final and definitive revelation of God to humanity. The author begins by establishing that "Long ago, at many times and in many ways" God spoke to his people (Heb. 1:1). But now, in these last days, God has conclusively spoken through Jesus—his beloved Son, the Creator, Sustainer, and Savior of the world (vv. 2–3), and an exact image of the Father (v. 3). The greatness of Jesus is finally depicted by his exaltation at the right hand of God above all earthly and heavenly beings (v. 4).

The Big Picture

Hebrews 1:1–4 draws our hearts to worship in light of the radiant majesty and unrivaled power of Jesus Christ.

> ## Reflection and Discussion

Read through the passage for this study, Hebrews 1:1–4. After reading the passage, reread the portions listed below and respond to the questions—first with regard to Jesus as divine revelation (vv. 1–2a), then on Jesus' person, work, and status (vv. 2b–4). (For further background, see the *ESV Study Bible*, page 2361, available online at esv.org.)

1. Jesus as Divine Revelation (1:1–2a)

God has spoken. In the introductory verses of Hebrews, the author sweeps over the span of God's progressive revelation and lands on Jesus Christ as the climax of his communication. Considering some of the miraculous ways God spoke to the patriarchs and prophets in the Old Testament, what is the author attempting to demonstrate by contrasting how God previously spoke, and how God, through his Son, has now definitively spoken to his people (1:1–2)?

In verses 1–2, the author of Hebrews contrasts revelation in the Old Testament with the finality of God's revelation in Jesus Christ in four areas. Compare the eras of revelation, the recipients of revelation, the agents of revelation, and the ways in which revelation was expressed.

Jesus is the definitive revelation of God in history. The implication of this truth is that God's revelation in the Old Testament was sufficient for that era but incomplete. How does the revelation of Jesus "in these last days" affect how we read the complete canon of Scripture (Luke 24:27; John 5:39–40)?

----

2. Jesus: Person, Work, and Status (1:2b–4)

Many scholars believe that the titles "Son" and "heir" applied to Jesus in Heb. 1:2 are allusions to Psalm 2:7–8, a royal coronation Psalm recalling God's pledge to David's heir in 2 Samuel 7:12–16. In ancient Israel it was the firstborn son who had the right of inheritance. By virtue of his royal sonship, Jesus is the heir of the universe, including the world to come (Heb. 2:5–9), a position of blessing and glory. What is the author highlighting in Jesus' unique relationship and responsibility concerning the universe?

In Hebrews 1:2–3, the author asserts that all of God's creation belongs to Jesus because it was through his agency that all things came into existence and through his power that the universe is upheld. The preexistence, authority, power, and full deity of Jesus are evident in his role in creating and upholding the universe (1:10; see John 1:3; 1 Cor. 8:6; Col. 1:16). What do these truths communicate to us about the purpose of creation and Jesus' dominion over his handiwork?

In Hebrews 1:3 Jesus is described as the "radiance of the glory of God." In biblical literature "glory" often refers to the luminous manifestation of God's person (see Ex. 16:7; 33:18; Isa. 40:5; 60:1, 19). Concerning the significance of the word "radiance," many have noted that the moon reflects light whereas the sun radiates light because it is its source. What does this tell us about Jesus as the radiance of God and our role as reflectors of God's glory?

Hebrews 1:3 proclaims that Jesus is "the exact imprint of God's nature." To the initial readers, this language would have been reminiscent of an impression placed as an image, as on a coin. Simply put, Jesus is the true image of God (2 Cor. 4:4; Col. 1:15). How do these words help us understand what Jesus taught in John 14:8–11?

After making purification for sins, Jesus sat down at "the right hand of God." Many scholars believe this is an overt allusion to Psalm 110:1. This Psalm is quoted directly in Hebrews 1:13 and alluded to at 8:1; 10:12; and 12:2. What is being communicated when the author writes that Christ "sat down at the right hand of God"?

Jesus is declared superior not only to the prophets but also to the angels[1] because of his more excellent inherited name (1:4). The author seems to be echoing 2 Samuel 7 concerning the honor conferred on Jesus as the Davidic heir. What is the significance of distinguishing Jesus from the angels in the position of the royal heir?

Read through the following three sections on *Gospel Glimpses, Whole-Bible Connections*, and *Theological Soundings*. Then take time to reflect on the *Personal Implications* these sections may have for your walk with the Lord.

▶ Gospel Glimpses

PURIFICATION OF SIN.[2] The Bible is clear that sin and its corruption have destructive implications for humanity and for all of creation. The need for purification from sin is part of the overarching storyline of the Bible. The cosmic scope of sin sets the stage for cosmic redemption by the atoning death of Jesus. In the Old Testament, atoning sacrifices were established for God's people to mediate punishment for their sin and obtain cleansing through blood (Leviticus 16). Atoning sacrifices also cleansed the objects of the earthly temple patterned after the cosmos, the temple dwelling of God. In Hebrews we see that the death of Jesus obtained the needed purification of sins and the cleansing of the human conscience before God (Heb. 1:3; 9:14). Jesus' sacrifice also extended to the purification of "heavenly things" (9:23) and is therefore cosmic in scope. The heart of the gospel is the good news that the blood of Jesus atoned for sin and has implications for the entire cosmos.

COMPLETE SALVATION. Right before Jesus took his last breath on the cross he proclaimed, "It is finished" (John 19:30). The work that the Father had sent him to accomplish was complete; namely, his perfect sacrifice for our sin was finished (Heb. 1:3; 9:11–12, 25–28). The author of Hebrews points out that once Jesus' work on the cross, and in the resurrection, was complete, he sat down at the right hand of God, underscoring the finality of his work and status. Unlike the Levitical priests who made imperfect sacrifices year after year to cover sins, Jesus made the perfect once-for-all sacrifice that eradicated sin—and then he took his seat to reign forever (10:11–12).

Whole-Bible Connections

REVELATION AND REDEMPTION. Revelation in human language is essential to the communication of God's redemptive plan through Jesus Christ. Without verbal revelation, humanity cannot have access to the good news of God's redemption. The revelation found in the Old Testament does not stand on its own, however; it is incomplete without its conclusion and fulfillment in Jesus Christ. "In these last days" we come to understand that the persons and institutions of the Old Testament point to the person and work of Jesus Christ, in whom we find redemption (Heb. 1:1–2).

THE PERFECT SON. In the Bible, sonship is related to familial likeness, lineage, and inheritance. Not only was God's first "son" Adam created in his image, Adam also bore sons in his own likeness, and thus in the image of God (Gen. 1:28; 5:1–3). God later refers to Israel as his corporate "son" (Ex. 4:22–23; Ps. 2:7; Hos. 11:1) and his "firstborn" (Deut. 33:17; Ps. 2:7; Jer. 31:9; Ezra 6:58). Both Adam and Israel failed to be what the Father desired. Both failed to do what God had required of them as "sons." Their disobedience contrasts starkly with the flawless obedience of Jesus, the divine-human son, who perfectly images the Father and brings him honor (Prov. 10:1; 15:20; 23:15).

GLORY OF GOD. In biblical language, the glory of God is an image of his perfection, beauty, and greatness. In Genesis 1:27 we are told that Adam was created in the image of God. As God's image-bearer, Adam, along with the rest of humanity, was created to reflect God's glory. But sin destroyed the pure reflection of God's glory in Adam and his children. Unmarred by sin, Jesus is declared the second, and last, Adam, who fully represents God's image and flawlessly radiates his glory (Rom. 5:12–21). Yet unlike Adam, Jesus is the exact imprint of God and is identical in substance to God (Heb. 1:3).

Theological Soundings

CREATION. The biblical story begins with a majestic description of how God created the heavens and earth to be his dwelling place and how it came to be inhabited by his creatures. In Hebrews 1:2–3 we are told that Jesus is not only the instrument of the original creative act in Genesis 1 but is also intimately involved in the continued care of creation (compare the description of Jesus in John 1:1–18). Jesus was the agent in whom and through whom the entire universe of space and time came into existence. As the image of God incarnate, Jesus is the point of contact between the Creator and his universe. He is the frame of reference for the original purpose and for the post-fall renewal of God's creation (Col. 1:15–23).

PROVIDENCE. The doctrine of providence teaches that God sustains the world he has created and directs it to his appointed purposes. In Hebrews 1:3 we see that God is personally involved with his creation in sustaining and preserving it. His providential dominion extends over all things in the universe; all of creation is sustained and carried forward by Jesus' powerful word. Moreover, Jesus came to provide the final and complete purification for sins.

Personal Implications

Take time to reflect on the implications of Hebrews 1:1–4 for your own life today. Make notes below on the personal implications for your walk with the Lord of the (1) *Gospel Glimpses*, (2) *Whole-Bible Connections*, (3) *Theological Soundings*, and (4) this passage as a whole.

1. Gospel Glimpses

2. Whole-Bible Connections

3. Theological Soundings

----

4. Hebrews 1:1–4

► As You Finish This Unit . . .

Take a moment now to ask for the Lord's blessing and help as you continue in this study of Hebrews. And take a moment also to look back through this unit of study, to reflect on some things that the Lord may be teaching you—and perhaps to highlight or underline these to review again in the future.

Definitions

[1] **Angel** – A supernatural messenger of God, often sent to carry out his will or to assist human beings in carrying out his will. Though angels are more powerful than humans and often instill awe, they are not to be worshiped (Col. 2:18; Rev. 22:8–9). The Bible does, however, note various appearances of an "angel of the Lord," apparently a physical manifestation of God himself.

[2] **Sin** – Any violation of or failure to adhere to the commands of God, or the desire to do so.

WEEK 3: JESUS IS SUPERIOR TO ANGELIC BEINGS

Hebrews 1:5–2:18

▲

The Place of the Passage

By a chain of Old Testament passages, Jesus is shown to be superior to the angels as the unique Son of God (Heb. 1:5–14). Because of his status as the Son of God, Jesus enjoys a unique relationship with the Father in position, nature, and authority. Jesus is also presented as the unique Son of Man, which establishes him as the true sacrifice for sin and introduces him as the sympathetic High Priest (2:1–18). This passage contains the first of five warnings in the book of Hebrews; here, we are warned to trust in the salvation provided through Jesus Christ.

The Big Picture

Hebrews 1:5–2:18 exalts Jesus above the angels as the unique Son of God who made propitiation[1] for the sins of humanity and now serves as the Mediator and High Priest between God and humanity.

> ### Reflection and Discussion

Read through the complete passage for this study, Hebrews 1:5–2:18. After reading the entire passage, begin by rereading the portions listed and responding to the questions below. (For further background, see the *ESV Study Bible*, pages 2361–2364, available online at esv.org.)

1. Jesus' Status as Eternal Son and King (1:5–14)

The author builds his support for the superiority of Jesus over the angels by stringing together various Old Testament texts to substantiate his argument. Jesus is shown as superior by the nature of his relationship to the Father (1:5), his position over the angels (vv. 6–7), and his kingly authority (vv. 8–9). How does the author's application of Old Testament texts to Jesus' sonship (Ps. 2:7; 2 Sam. 7:14), position (Ps. 97:7; 104:4), and authority (Ps. 45:6–7) fortify our faith in Jesus today?

By quoting Psalm 102:25–27 in Hebrews 1:10–12, the author emphasizes Jesus' role in creation and his eternal nature. How do Jesus' role in creation and his eternal lordship over creation embolden our allegiance to him?

In Hebrews 1:13 the writer applies Psalm 110:1 to Jesus, showing him as exalted to the right hand of God, a position of privilege and power (see Heb. 1:3). This particular psalm refers to the king's enthronement and victory over all of his enemies. What does Jesus' posture of being *seated* communicate about God's purposes in the life, death, and resurrection of Christ?

According to verse 14, angels are ministering spirits tasked with serving those who are to inherit salvation. How does the angels' role speak to the glory of the gospel and to the authority of Jesus Christ?

---

2. Warning One: Against Neglecting Salvation (2:1–4)

The author bolsters the reliability of the Mosaic law by the fact that it was given by the angels (Heb. 2:2; see also Deut. 33:2). If the Mosaic law came with retribution for disobedience, how much more recompense comes for those who reject salvation attested by God the Father and God the Son, and confirmed by signs, wonders, and miracles (Heb. 2:3–4)? Moreover, why should we be careful not to drift away from the gospel of grace[2] and consciously neglect its application for our lives (2:1)?

---

3. Jesus as the Founder of Salvation (2:5–18)

Hebrews 2:5–9 states that the present world and the world to come are subject to Jesus Christ. However, at the present time believers do not clearly see Jesus' supreme rule over the cosmos. Moreover, humans are temporarily lower in status and authority than the angels, in light of the fall and of man's failure to uphold the creation mandate (Gen. 1:28). How does Jesus, as the true representative of humanity, fulfill God's command to place everything in creation under subjection (Heb. 2:8)?

In Hebrews 2:10–13, the author cites Psalm 22:22 and Isaiah 8:17b–18 to show that the followers of the one unique Son of God are now also called "sons," for they are adopted into the newly redeemed human family through Jesus' perfect life and sacrifice. What are the benefits of being a son of God, or brother of Jesus Christ (see Gal. 4:1–7)?

In Hebrews 2:14–18 we see the solidarity Jesus has with humanity in that he took on "flesh and blood." However, unlike what any other human could have done, Jesus stormed the gates of death, defeated the Evil One, and liberated us from slavery to death (vv. 14–16). How then do verses 17–18 provide believers hope amid spiritual infirmities?

Read through the following three sections on *Gospel Glimpses*, *Whole-Bible Connections*, and *Theological Soundings*. Then take time to reflect on the *Personal Implications* these sections may have for your walk with the Lord.

▶ Gospel Glimpses

RELIABLE GOSPEL. The danger of neglecting the gospel of Jesus Christ is heightened by its superiority to prior revelation, which came through prophets and angels (Heb. 1:2; 2:2). According to reliable eyewitnesses, Jesus himself first announced his good news (2:3). Moreover, God confirmed this good news proclaimed by Jesus with signs, wonders, miracles, and gifts of the Holy Spirit (Acts 2:22; 2 Cor. 12:12; Heb. 2:4). The gospel is not only good news; it is *reliable* good news—good news that is worth staking our lives on.

THE GOOD KING. In the first century, "gospel" ("good news") was used regularly to refer to the birth, announcement, accession, or victory of a great king. According to Hebrews 1:8, Jesus is the eternal messianic King whose rein will never end. Unlike the Davidic kings of the past, his rule is not hindered by frailty. Jesus' rule is marked by perfect justice and righteousness. Jesus' kingly rule is also good in that he delivers, sanctifies, and cares for his people (1:8; 2:6, 9–18). Lastly, unlike any other king in history, Jesus will reign forever and ever as King of kings (Rev. 5:9–14).

DRANK DEEPLY OF DEATH. As the perfect sacrifice, Jesus tasted death on behalf of everyone who believes (Heb. 2:9). Even more so, Jesus drank the cup of God's wrath to the bitter dregs in order to consume the wrath of God on behalf of believers, thus destroying the death grip of the Devil (2:14–15, 17). In Christ there is no fear in death, only hope in life. On the cross Jesus did away with the power of death. In his powerful resurrection, Jesus sealed the promise of new eternal life.

▶ Whole-Bible Connections

PROMISED KING. In Hebrews 1:5b, the author echoes the proclamation made by King David concerning his covenant heir, whom God will designate as his own Son (2 Sam. 7:14; 1 Chron. 17:13). In the context of 2 Samuel this is surely Solomon. While these words were never realized in Solomon, they have found their fulfillment in Jesus, who is the true and greater Davidic King whose kingdom is established forever (2 Sam. 7:16). Therefore, the kingly dominion that the Israelite kings foreshadowed, but failed to uphold as God's representatives on earth, finds its fulfillment in Jesus (Heb. 2:8–9; Rev. 3:21). The Old Testament kings are the shadows; Jesus is the substance. Jesus is the eternal King of kings whose perfect rule and justice will never end.

SPIRITUAL EXODUS. The author of Hebrews refers to Jesus not only as the founder of salvation,[3] but also as the One who brings the new covenant people into glory (Heb. 2:10). Some Bible versions translate "founder" as "pioneer." The imagery of Jesus pioneering our salvation looks back in the Old Testament to those who led the Israelites through the wilderness and also into battle (Num. 10:4; 13:2–3; Judg. 5:15; 9:44, 11:6–11; 1 Chron. 5:24; 26:26; 2 Chron. 23:14; Neh. 2:9). As his people's forerunner and representative, Jesus has entered the presence of God to secure their entry there; he has become the way for them to enter the promised rest of God. Jesus is the true and greater Moses who delivers all of his people into God's rest.

PROPITIATION. The word "propitiation" conveys the sense of an atoning sacrifice that satisfies the wrath of God against sin (Rom. 3:25; Heb. 2:17). Throughout redemption history, God's righteous anger is shown as needing to be appeased before the sin of God's people could be forgiven. The final propitiation by Christ, making full payment for sin once and for all, is foreshadowed several times in the Old Testament (Ex. 32:11–14; Num. 25:8; Josh. 7:25–26). Where the Old Testament sacrifices failed, Jesus succeeded in once for all propitiating God's wrath against the sin of his people.

▶ Theological Soundings

ANGELS. According to the Scriptures, angels are majestic created beings that function primarily as worshipers and messengers of God, revealing his will and announcing key events throughout redemptive history (Dan. 9:20–27; Luke 1:11–20; Acts 7:38; Heb. 2:2). Angels also minister to God's people (1 Kings 19:5–7; Ps. 91:11; Heb. 1:14). The splendor of angels serves as a reference point from which the author of Hebrews can speak of the much higher position of the exalted Son (1:5–13). The angels' worship of Christ as he enters the heavenly realm solidifies his superior position (v. 6). Though angels are beautiful and powerful beings, Christ's beauty and power surpasses theirs exponentially.

HUMANITY OF JESUS. While on earth, Jesus was made lower than the angels as the incarnate God-man by sharing fully in human flesh and blood (Heb. 2:9, 14). Christ's humanity was necessary so that he could endure temptation and suffering and thus could serve as the one true sacrifice for sin. Unless Jesus became human in every respect (except for sin), experiencing the full range of temptation, he could not serve as the sympathetic High Priest who knows man's spiritual infirmities.

MIRACLES. In the Bible, miracles are God's non-normative acts of power by which he bears witness to himself and authenticates his messengers and message (John 2:11; 3:2; Acts 2:22). In the early church, the apostles and others also performed miracles, to confirm the validity of the gospel message they proclaimed (Acts 2:43; 3:6–10; 4:30; 8:6–8, 13; 9:40–42). In Hebrews 2:3–4, we read that God confirmed the message of salvation himself by signs and wonders.

> ## Personal Implications

Take time to reflect on the implications of Hebrews 1:5–2:18 for your own life today. Make notes below on the personal implications for your walk with the Lord of the (1) *Gospel Glimpses*, (2) *Whole-Bible Connections*, (3) *Theological Soundings*, and (4) this passage as a whole.

1. Gospel Glimpses

2. Whole-Bible Connections

3. Theological Soundings

4. Hebrews 1:5–2:18

As You Finish This Unit . . .

Take a moment now to ask for the Lord's blessing and help as you continue in this study of Hebrews. Take a moment also to look back through this unit of study, to reflect on some things that the Lord may be teaching you—and perhaps to highlight or underline these to review again in the future.

Definitions

[1] **Propitiation** – The appeasement of wrath by the offering of a gift or sacrifice. Jesus made propitiation for the sins of humanity by his suffering and death (Rom. 3:25; Heb. 2:17; 1 John 2:2; 4:10).

[2] **Grace** – Unmerited favor, especially the free gift of salvation that God gives to believers through faith in Jesus Christ.

[3] **Salvation** – Deliverance from the eternal consequences of sin. Jesus' death and resurrection purchased eternal salvation for believers (Rom. 1:16).

WEEK 4: JESUS IS SUPERIOR TO MOSES

Hebrews 3:1–4:13

▲

The Place of the Passage

In Hebrews 3:1–6 Jesus is shown to be superior to Moses, one of God's most faithful servants. Jesus is worthy of supreme glory in that he is the faithful High Priest and Son of God. The author exhorts the Christians to respond with faithfulness and perseverance to God's redemptive work (3:7–4:13). In this section, readers receive their second warning, namely, to persevere in the faith, unlike the exodus generation, who hardened their hearts (3:7–18).

The Big Picture

Hebrews 3:1–4:13 shows Jesus Christ as the Apostle and perfect Son sent to serve as the faithful High Priest.

Reflection and Discussion

Read through the complete passage for this study, Hebrews 3:1–4:13. After reading the entire passage, begin by rereading the portions listed and responding to the questions below. (For further background, see the *ESV Study Bible*, pages 2365–2367, available online at esv.org.)

1. Jesus Is Greater Than Moses (3:1–6)

In Heb. 3:1–2 Jesus is confessed as the Apostle sent to bring deliverance and as the High Priest making atonement for the sins of God's people. As holy members of God's family, what does it mean to "share in a heavenly calling" (v. 1)? How can Jesus' faithfulness embolden us to hold fast in confidence and in hope to our heavenly calling (v. 6)?

Moses was a faithful servant in the house of God in spite of the Israelites' faithlessness (Num. 12:7). However, Jesus is worthy of more glory than Moses because of his perfect faithfulness as the Son who not only presides over but also *built* the house of God (1 Chron. 17:14–17; Heb. 3:1–6). For the original audience, who were familiar with the Old Testament, what was the significance of the author comparing Jesus to Moses? What can we learn from Moses' faithfulness as a member of the house of God?

2. Warning Two: The Failure of the Exodus Generation (3:7–19)

After exploring the contrast between Moses' and Jesus' faithfulness, the author now turns to the responses of their followers by citing Psalm 95:7–11. The author warns against the unbelief of a sinful hardened heart causing one to fall away (Heb. 3:7–12). How do these strong words help keep us from living in rebellion? How does this passage enlighten us on the difference between genuine faith and false faith?

In Hebrews 3:13–14 the author explains how mutual encouragement and accountability can be the antidote to the corrosion of unbelief. How does heeding the exhortation to mutual commitment in sharing Christ keep Christians resolved to persevere to the end?

In Hebrews 3:15, the author returns to Psalm 95:7–8 and reminds the readers of the exodus generation's failures (3:16–19; see Ex. 17:1–7; Num. 14:20–38). How does the exodus generation's unbelief and failure to enter God's rest point to both the warning of falling away and the hope we have in Jesus Christ?

3. Entering God's Rest (4:1–13)

God's deliverance of the Israelites and their hope of entering the Promised Land foreshadowed the work of Jesus. For the church, the promised rest of

God has been inaugurated in the resurrection of Christ and is awaiting consummation in his second coming; however the author fears that some will not enter that rest (Heb. 4:1). According to 4:1–3 how does faith relate to entering the promised rest of God?

In Hebrews 4:4, the author speaks of entering God's rest in relation to the seventh day of creation (Gen. 2:2) and notes that the Israelites ultimately failed to enter the rest of God (Heb. 4:5–9). Taken together, God's Sabbath[1] rest that began in Genesis 2 is still open and can be entered. What does it mean to enter and rest from one's works[2] as God did from his (Heb. 4:10)?

After calling the readers to strive to enter God's rest in perseverance, the author reminds them that faithless disobedience will not go unnoticed (Heb. 4:11–13). Knowing that God's Word acts as an agent revealing one's innermost thoughts and intentions, how can we use his Word to fight disobedience and unbelief?

Read through the following three sections on *Gospel Glimpses*, *Whole-Bible Connections*, and *Theological Soundings*. Then take time to reflect on the *Personal Implications* these sections may have for your walk with the Lord.

▶ Gospel Glimpses

PERSEVERING FAITH. Those who exhibit persevering faith will not fall away in unbelief (Heb. 3:14). Self-examination combined with gospel faith guards from developing a hardened heart. Therefore, we should be watchful and hold on to our original confidence in the gospel of Jesus Christ to the end, using God's Word to reveal any unbelief or disobedience (vv. 12–13). Perseverance in the faith is one means of assurance that believers have in the Christian life (v. 6). Thankfully, it is the grace of God that saves us and sustains us until the end.

SABBATH REST. In the gospel, God gives Sabbath rest to his people (Heb. 4:9–10). In the creation account we read that God rested on the seventh day because his work was complete (Gen. 2:2). Humanity imitates the pattern of God's work and rest in the sabbath cycle (Ex. 20:8–11; Leviticus 25). The sabbath points forward to the rest that Christ achieved with his resurrection and ascension (Heb. 10:12–13). Christians enter a deep rest of the soul in confessing that Jesus' work of redemption was complete when he declared, "It is finished," and then when he rose from the dead (John 19:30; 20:19). The church now awaits Jesus' second coming, at which time God's rest will be fully manifested (Rev. 22:3–5). Until that day, believers are called to rest in Christ's salvation and resist the temptation to fall back into works righteousness (Gal. 2:16; 3:10–14).

▶ Whole-Bible Connections

FAITHFUL SERVANT. Moses faithfully fulfilled God's appointed roles as deliverer from slavery in Egypt, exodus leader, and lawgiver (Ex. 3:10; Deut. 18:15–19). Jesus is greater than Moses in that he delivers his people from the greater slavery of sin and death, and into the promised eternal rest of God.

THE SON OF MAN. The title Jesus uses more than any other to refer to himself is "the Son of Man" (e.g., Matt. 8:20; 11:19). While labeling himself this way may underscore Jesus' humanity, the phrase is most significant in relation to the figure in Daniel 7 who receives supreme authority and an everlasting kingdom from God (see Dan. 7:13–14; Matt. 26:64; Mark 14:62). And, as the perfect Son, Jesus faithfully upholds the entirety of the law, enabling him to serve as High Priest and everlasting King (Heb. 3:1–6).

EXODUS TO PROMISE. The exodus generation failed to enter the rest of God (the Promised Land) due to their unbelief and disobedience (Num. 14:20–24; 20:12). The pattern of the exodus is repeated in the church's deliverance from sin and death and in its future deliverance to the promised eternal rest of God. Unlike the exodus generation, Jesus is the true Israelite whose faithfulness to

God is perfect. Unlike Moses and Joshua, Jesus is able to sustain and deliver every last one of his people to the promised rest of God (4:1–16).

Theological Soundings

HOUSE OF GOD. Like other metaphors for the people of God, "house" refers to the corporate identity of the church as God's dwelling place (1 Cor. 3:16; 6:19; 2 Cor. 6:16; 1 Tim. 3:15; 1 Pet. 2:5). Jesus holds a privileged place in God's house as Son (Heb. 3:6), builder (3:3–4), and chief cornerstone (Eph. 2:20–21). The household of God is united by faith and exhorted to encourage one another toward faith, obedience, and perseverance.

WORD OF GOD. The Bible is a divine-human Word, given to us by God through human beings within redemptive history, who testify about who God is and what he has done. The Bible is God's personal utterance to us, acting as God himself, searching and exposing our hearts. Through God's written Word, his people may expose error, grow in Christlikeness, and gain understanding as to what it means to live a life pleasing to God (Heb. 4:12; 2 Tim. 3:16).

Personal Implications

Take time to reflect on the implications of Hebrews 3:1–4:13 for your own life today. Make notes below on the personal implications for your walk with the Lord of the (1) *Gospel Glimpses*, (2) *Whole-Bible Connections*, (3) *Theological Soundings*, and (4) this passage as a whole.

1. Gospel Glimpses

2. Whole-Bible Connections

3. Theological Soundings

---

4. Hebrews 3:1–4:13

► As You Finish This Unit . . .

Take a moment now to ask for the Lord's blessing and help as you continue in this study of Hebrews. And take a moment also to look back through this unit of study, to reflect on some things that the Lord may be teaching you—and perhaps to highlight or underline these to review again in the future.

Definitions

[1] **Sabbath** – Saturday, the seventh day of the week, the Jewish day of worship and rest (Gen. 2:2–3; Ex. 31:13–17). Christians meet for worship on Sunday, the day of Christ's resurrection (Acts 20:7), and regard Sunday, rather than Saturday, as their weekly day of rest. And yet, believers look forward to an eternal Sabbath rest (Heb. 4:1–13).

[2] **Works** – Actions and attitudes, either good or bad. True faith in Christ will inevitably produce good works that are pleasing to God. Good works can never be the basis or means of salvation, which is by grace through faith alone.

WEEK 5: JESUS IS THE SUPERIOR HIGH PRIEST, PART 1

Hebrews 4:14–5:10

The Place of the Passage

The author now builds on the themes first introduced in Hebrews 2:17–3:12. He proclaims Jesus as the holy and sympathetic High Priest appointed by God the Father. Moreover, Christ is to suffer for the sake of others so that they may receive the gift of eternal salvation (4:14–5:10). Faithfulness is the proper response to all that Christ has done for us.

The Big Picture

Hebrews 4:14–5:10 exalts Jesus Christ, the sinless Son of God, as the appointed sympathetic High Priest in the order of Melchizedek.

> ## Reflection and Discussion

Read through the complete passage for this study, Hebrews 4:14–5:10. After reading the entire passage, begin by rereading the portions listed and responding to the questions below. (For further background, see the *ESV Study Bible*, pages 2367–2368, available online at esv.org.)

1. Jesus, the Great High Priest (4:14–5:10)

The author announced Jesus' role as High Priest in Hebrews 2:17; here in 4:14–16, Jesus' High Priestly role is explained further. Jesus has "passed through the heavens" and is now seated at the right hand of God (1:13; 4:14). Our great High Priest is not only the divine Son—God himself—he is also fully human and able to sympathize with us (4:15). In what unique ways is Jesus able to sympathize with us, inasmuch as he is intimately familiar with both heaven and earth?

According to this passage, the high priest must be called by God to his office, and must be able to sympathize with those whom he represents. Knowing that Jesus is our great High Priest, how does this enable us to hold firmly to our faith?

The author exhorts the reader to draw near to the throne of grace with confidence in order to find mercy[1] and help in times of need (Heb. 4:16). Though we still struggle with indwelling sin, through Christ God's holy throne becomes a throne of grace. How does this give us incentive for both prayer and praise? Why are Christians able to speak honestly before God without fear of condemnation?

High priests[2] receive their call and charge from God Almighty. According to Hebrews 5:1–2, what is the essential purpose of the high priest? In what ways do Jesus' life and work fulfill the high priestly criteria (vv. 1–2, 5)? In what way is Jesus different from and greater than former high priests (v. 3)?

In Hebrews 5:5–6 the writer recalls Psalm 2:7 again and Psalm 110 to speak of Christ as the Son and eternal High Priest in the order of Melchizedek. Why is Jesus compared to Melchizedek (Gen. 14:18–20)?

During his life on earth, Jesus offered up intense, heartfelt, reverent, and submissive prayers to God the Father, with loud cries and tears (Heb. 5:7; see, e.g., Luke 22:39–46). Jesus' perfect obedience formed the basis for his prayers being answered (Heb. 5:8). How can we learn from, and more important, lean on Christ's perfect prayer life in times of struggle?

Hebrews 5:8–9 explains that Jesus learned obedience through what he suffered, and was thus made perfect. Essentially, Jesus was "made perfect" in the sense that he became qualified through his perfect obedience to be the source of salvation to all believers (v. 9). How can the experience and perfection of Jesus give us hope when we lack the obedience that God desires?

Read through the following three sections on *Gospel Glimpses*, *Whole-Bible Connections*, and *Theological Soundings*. Then take time to reflect on the *Personal Implications* these sections may have for your walk with the Lord.

▶ Gospel Glimpses

TEMPTED WITHOUT SIN. Temptation can be seen as intended to bring us down, or it can be seen as a test to build us up in sanctification (Matt. 4:1–11; Luke 22:28). Jesus was tempted in every area of life, yet unlike every other human, he remained sinless. Christians can find comfort in the fact that Jesus can sympathize with them in temptation, and in knowing that Jesus remained perfectly faithful and obedient where they find themselves giving in to sin (Heb. 4:15). More important, when we give in to temptation we are not finally condemned by God. Christ's perfect obedience has been imputed to us, and we will be drawn to repentance through his Spirit, and by his grace we will be forgiven.

THRONE OF GRACE. A throne is an image of authority, majesty, and power. God's throne is a holy throne (Ps. 47:8) and is a place of judgment and condemnation of sin. However, because of the finished work of Christ on the cross, Christians are called to boldly draw near to God's throne. With Jesus seated at his right hand (Heb. 4:16; 8:1; 12:2) making intercession for the saints (7:25; 10:22), God the Father graciously provides forgiveness for sin and empowers Christians with strength to overcome temptation (2:18). In humility and confidence we can confess our sin, knowing that God will forgive us and show us grace.

ETERNAL SALVATION. Jesus' perfect obedience (Heb. 5:8; 7:26–28) and sacrifice provides the basis for salvation by grace through faith. Salvation through Christ is eternal (2:10; 9:23–28) because Jesus' sacrifice was made once for all (10:12). As believers, we are held by Christ and sealed with the Spirit until the last day (John 10:28; 2 Cor. 1:22). On the last day, Christ will claim those who are his before the Father in heaven (Rev. 3:5).

Whole-Bible Connections

HIGH PRIEST. In the Mosaic priesthood, the Levitical high priest served as the religious head of his people and mediator between God and man. The high priest was the only one permitted to enter the inner part of the temple where God dwelt, to make atonement for his people (Ex. 26:33; Leviticus 16). By offering the perfect sacrifice for sin the true and greater High Priest, Jesus, opened the way for all of God's people to enter the fullness of God's presence (Heb. 7:27). While the Levitical priests were temporary, Jesus serves as the permanent and eternal High Priest (7:23–24). Because of Christ's work, we are always able to confidently draw near to God (4:14–16).

MELCHIZEDEK. Melchizedek was a "king-priest"—King of Salem and priest of God in the time of Abraham (Gen. 14:17–20; Ps. 110:4). Melchizedek serves as a type for Jesus as king-priest. Melchizedek's name is interpreted to mean "king of righteousness," and his title as king of Salem to mean "king of peace," foreshadowing Jesus' reign of righteousness and peace (Heb. 7:1–10).

Theological Soundings

JESUS' LIMITATIONS. The humanity of the Son of God brought him certain limitations. He was born as a helpless infant and grew into adulthood, just like the rest of us (Luke 2:7; 2:40, 52). He became tired and hungry just as all humans do (John 4:6; 19:28; Matt. 4:2). Jesus also had the full range of human emotions. Before his crucifixion, as he faced the reality of being slaughtered for the sins of mankind, his soul was sorrowful, even to death (Matt. 26:38). His heart was often full of emotion as he prayed to the Father (Heb. 5:7). Jesus grew in moral strength throughout his life as he completed the work his Father had sent him to accomplish. In all of this, he remained without sin (Heb. 4:15; 5:8).

PERSONAL GOD. The God of the Bible is not an abstract deity removed from his creation; he is a personal God who relates to his creation and sympathizes with his people. This is most clearly seen in the incarnation of Jesus Christ. In Hebrews 4:15–16 we are reminded that Jesus' humanity also enables him to sympathize with us as our High Priest. Because of his humanity, Jesus is able to know by experience the temptations and struggles of our lives, and therefore is able to sympathize with us and help us when we are tempted (Heb. 2:18). Jesus has now entered into the presence of God, and by his presence there he pleads on our behalf (9:24–28).

Personal Implications

Take time to reflect on the implications of Hebrews 4:14–5:10 for your own life today. Make notes below on the personal implications for your walk with the Lord of the (1) *Gospel Glimpses*, (2) *Whole-Bible Connections*, (3) *Theological Soundings*, and (4) this passage as a whole.

1. Gospel Glimpses

2. Whole-Bible Connections

3. Theological Soundings

4. Hebrews 4:14–5:10

As You Finish This Unit . . .

Take a moment now to ask for the Lord's blessing and help as you continue in this study of Hebrews. And take a moment also to look back through this unit of study, to reflect on some things that the Lord may be teaching you—and perhaps to highlight or underline these to review again in the future.

Definitions

[1] **Mercy** – Compassion and kindness toward someone experiencing hardship, sometimes even when such suffering results from the person's own sin or foolishness. God displays mercy toward his people and they, in turn, are called to display mercy toward others (Luke 6:36).

[2] **Priest** – In Old Testament Israel, the priest represented the people before God and represented God before the people. Only those descended from Aaron could be priests. Their prescribed duties also included inspecting and receiving sacrifices from the people and overseeing the daily activities and maintenance of the tabernacle or temple.

WEEK 6: A WARNING
AGAINST APOSTASY

Hebrews 5:11–6:20

The Place of the Passage

Interrupting the exposition of Jesus' role as High Priest (Heb. 4:14–5:10; 7:1–8:13), the author suddenly challenges readers to move beyond the basics of the faith toward spiritual maturity (5:11–6:3). He concludes by exhorting them and showing confidence in their ability to persevere, using Abraham as an example of "faithful faith" (6:9–20). The third of five warning passages appears in 6:4–8, warning the readers of the danger of falling away.

The Big Picture

Hebrews 5:11–6:20 glorifies God by pointing to Jesus Christ as the forerunner, anchor, and High Priest of our faith.

Reflection and Discussion

Read through the complete passage for this study, Hebrews 5:11–6:20. After reading the entire passage, begin by rereading the portions listed and responding to the questions below. (For further background, see the *ESV Study Bible*, pages 2368–2370, available online at esv.org.)

1. Warning Three: Against Apostasy (5:11–6:12)

In Heb. 5:11–12 the author scolds the readers for their immaturity in the faith, for, he says, they have become "dull of hearing" (v. 11) and do not have a solid grasp on the fundamental truths of God (v. 12). What are some possible reasons for their mental laziness and unwillingness to work out the deeper implications of the gospel in their lives?

At this point in their faith, the original audience should have matured enough to instruct others in "the basic principles of the oracles of God," which he also refers to as the "word of righteousness" (Heb. 5:12–13). What is the author referring to by "basic principles" and fundamental "oracles" of God (see 6:1–2; Acts 7:38; Rom. 3:2)?

In comparison to those who are infants in the faith, the mature believer is characterized as well-learned and well-practiced in the faith (Heb. 5:14). Why are both doctrine and practice important for maturing a believer?

The author indicates that he is committed to moving the readers from immaturity to maturity in their faith (Heb. 6:3). In 6:1–2 we see three pairs of basic principles:

1. *Faith and repentance:* Repenting[1] of sin and turning from trusting in one's own works to resting on the finished work of Christ are the marks of Christian conversion (Heb. 6:12; 9:14; 10:22, 38–39; 12:2; 13:7).
2. *Washings and laying on of hands:* These distinctive initiatory rites indicate that one is becoming an active part of the church (Acts 6:6; 8:14–17; 9:12–19; 19:5–6).
3. *Resurrection and eternal judgment:* Christians have a future hope in the resurrection. They are safe in Christ from the eternal judgment that awaits nonbelievers (Heb. 9:27; 10:27; 11:19, 35).

Why are these principles important for helping someone move toward maturity in the faith?

In Hebrews 6:4–7, the writer notes that some of the original audience have participated in the Christian church and have shared in her blessings, but either are at risk of falling or have already fallen away from the faith (it is not clear which he means). Moreover, he says that it is impossible to restore such people again to repentance, because they are willfully rejecting Christ. Describe what the author means when charging those who have "fallen away" with showing contempt for Christ and making him contemptible in the eyes of others (vv. 6–7).

Is it possible to be enlightened by God's Word concerning salvation, to appear to display Spirit-wrought repentance of sin, and even to demonstrate signs of conversion, and still fail to persevere in the faith (vv. 4–6)? Why is it impossible to restore such people to repentance (vv. 6–7)?

The author uses the agricultural illustration in verse 7 so that the readers may heed his call to perseverance and patience (vv. 11–12). How does faith in salvation and a life of serving others (vv. 10–11) kindle perseverance and hope in the promises of God? What are the better things that accompany salvation (v. 9)?

2. The Certainty of God's Promise (6:13–20)

In verses 13–15, the writer offers Abraham as an example of one who, through patience and faith, inherited the promises of God (Gen. 22:16–17). In what ways does this passage encourage believers to imitate Abraham's patience in inheriting the promise of God?

In ancient times, oaths[2] required an appeal to a higher authority. In this passage it is said that God swore his promise with an oath to confirm his trustworthiness (Heb. 6:16–18). In what ways does this generate hope and confidence in the reader for holding fast to God's word?

While the author warns readers of falling away from the faith, he also anchors their assurance of salvation in Jesus Christ (6:19–20). What is the importance of the Old Testament references in this passage in solidifying Jesus as the manifestation of hope for the people of God (Matt. 27:51; Heb. 9:3; 10:20)?

Read through the following three sections on *Gospel Glimpses*, *Whole-Bible Connections*, and *Theological Soundings*. Then take time to reflect on the *Personal Implications* these sections may have for your walk with the Lord.

Gospel Glimpses

IN CHRIST ALONE. It is impossible to lead someone to repentance when he or she continues to reject the gospel. Those who reject Christ have turned from the only basis on which hope of salvation can be extended (Matt. 12:31–32; Heb. 6:4). Those who thus commit apostasy show contempt for Jesus, and in rejecting him they place themselves in the position of those who have cruci-fied him. In other words, apostates cause the shame of the cross to be reen-acted (v. 6). While we all face judgment and condemnation because of our sinfulness, by the grace of God salvation is available to us in Christ—and in him alone.

SALVIFIC OATH OF GOD. In ancient times the primary purpose of an oath was to confirm what had been said, thus putting an end to all argument (Heb. 6:16–18); those who took oaths were liable to judgment should they break them (Deut. 23:21–23). God swore by himself to Abraham concerning the heirs of his promise (Heb. 6:13; Genesis 15). Therefore, the promise of salvation through Jesus' High Priesthood is supremely trustworthy (Heb. 6:19–20). God's saving plan is unchangeable. Accordingly, believers have the strongest reason to hold fast to God's word of salvation.

Whole-Bible Connections

ABRAHAM'S PROMISE. God promised Abraham offspring that would be innumerable (Heb. 2:16; Gen. 12:1–3; 17:4–21; 18:17–19). It wasn't until a quarter of a century later that Isaac was born (Gen. 21:1–7). Every hope for fulfillment of God's promise to Abraham regarding his descendants hung upon Isaac, and it was Isaac whom Abraham was commanded to offer up as a sacrifice—though a ram was finally provided in his place. The full realization of the promise was found in Jesus, the descendant who would be offered as a sacrifice to secure the salvation for Abraham's offspring, thus blessing all the nations of the earth (Gen. 22:16–18).

FALLING AWAY. The description in Hebrews 6:4–6 of falling away evokes the context of Israel's wilderness journey and lack of perseverance. Israel expe-rienced the divine gift of God's provision through manna in the wilderness (Ex. 16:4); nevertheless they failed to enter the Promised Land because of their unbelief. In the same way, many have experienced the blessings of the new covenant yet spiritually "turn back to Egypt" and forfeit eternal rest. Be warned: those who finally fall away may give many external signs of faith before they abandon Christ (Heb. 6:7–8). To "fall away" from God leads to death and eternal judgment (3:12; 12:15).

Theological Soundings

SUFFICIENCY OF SCRIPTURE. The Bible is sufficient and profitable for the doctrinal instruction needed for godly living (Ps. 19:7–9; 2 Tim. 3:16–17). The readers to whom Hebrews 5:11–14 is addressed are infants in doctrine because of their laziness and unwillingness to work out the deeper implications of God's Word in their lives. However, the author's goal is that the readers would move to maturity through doctrinal development and scriptural examples (6:1–12).

UNPARDONABLE SIN. In the gospel accounts Jesus speaks of the unpardonable sin, namely, blasphemy against the Holy Spirit[3] (Matt. 12:31–32; Mark 3:29; Luke 12:10). In Hebrews 6:4–6, the author speaks of those who have experienced conviction of the truth and have tasted the goodness of God, and yet willfully turn away from Jesus. While being convinced of the truth of the gospel, they continually and deliberately defy the Holy Spirit's work attesting to that gospel (compare 10:26–27).

Personal Implications

Take time to reflect on the implications of Hebrews 5:11–6:20 for your own life today. Make notes below on the personal implications for your walk with the Lord of the (1) *Gospel Glimpses*, (2) *Whole-Bible Connections*, (3) *Theological Soundings*, and (4) this passage as a whole.

1. Gospel Glimpses

2. Whole-Bible Connections

3. Theological Soundings

> (blank lines for notes)

4. Hebrews 5:11–6:20

> (blank lines for notes)

> ### As You Finish This Unit . . .

Take a moment now to ask for the Lord's blessing and help as you continue in this study of Hebrews. And take a moment also to look back through this unit of study, to reflect on some key things that the Lord may be teaching you—and perhaps to highlight or underline these to review again in the future.

Definitions

[1] **Repentance** – A complete change of heart and mind regarding one's overall attitude toward God and/or one's individual actions. True regeneration and conversion is always accompanied by repentance.

[2] **Oath** – God's people were warned in the Old Testament not to swear promises rashly or falsely (Lev. 5:4; 19:11–12). Sometimes oaths were made in God's name, as though to guarantee them, but Jesus told his disciples not to swear oaths at all. Rather, they should let their simple statement of "yes" mean yes and their "no" mean no (Matt. 5:33–37). God's own oath, however, is an ultimate and unchallengeable guarantee (Heb. 6:13–20).

[3] **Holy Spirit** – One of the persons of the Trinity, fully God. The Bible mentions several roles of the Holy Spirit, including convicting people of sin, bringing them to conversion, indwelling them and empowering them to live in righteousness and faithfulness, supporting them in times of trial, and enabling them to understand the Scriptures. The Holy Spirit inspired the writers of Scripture, guiding them to record the very words of God. The Holy Spirit was especially active in Jesus' life and ministry on earth (e.g., Luke 3:22).

WEEK 7: JESUS IS THE SUPERIOR HIGH PRIEST, PART 2

Hebrews 7:1–8:13

The Place of the Passage

One of the central theological arguments of Hebrews is that Jesus Christ is the superior High Priest, in the order of Melchizedek (Heb. 5:1–10). In 7:1–28 the author picks up this argument again and delineates the nature of Jesus' priesthood in order to establish that it is superior to the Levitical priesthood. Jesus ministers in the greater heavenly tabernacle and has enacted better promises in the new covenant[1] (8:1–13).

The Big Picture

Hebrews 7:1–8:13 exhibits Jesus as the eternal Son and High Priest in the order of Melchizedek who ministers in heaven, allowing believers to draw near to God under the new covenant.

▶ **Reflection and Discussion**

Read through the complete passage for this study, Hebrews 7:1–8:13. After reading the entire passage, begin by rereading the portions listed and responding to the questions below. (For further background, see the *ESV Study Bible*, pages 2370–2373, available online at esv.org.)

1. The Priestly Order of Melchizedek (7:1–10)

Drawing on Genesis 14:18–20, the author describes the uniqueness of the king of Salem and priest Melchizedek (Heb. 7:1–3; see also Ps. 110:4). Based on Melchizedek's name and title, and the omission in Genesis of any genealogical qualification for the office of high priest (compare Num. 3:10, 15–16), in what ways does Melchizedek point forward to the life and ministry of Jesus Christ?

According to the author of Hebrews, Melchizedek was made (that is, biblically presented) in the likeness of the Son of God and so in Scripture remains a priest of the Most High God forever (Heb. 7:3). How does the author use this information to explain the purpose and function of Jesus' priestly ministry?

In Hebrews 7:4–10, the promise bearer and patriarch Abraham gave Melchizedek a tenth of his spoils (7:2; Gen. 14:20; Num. 18:21). As an inferior, however, Abraham then received a blessing from the hands of his superior Melchizedek, showing the eternal Melchizedek priesthood to be greater than the Levitical priesthood that would descend from Abraham (Heb. 7:4–8).

Following the argument from 7:4–10, how is the author building the case for Jesus' superiority as King and High Priest?

---

2. Jesus Compared to Melchizedek (7:11–28)

In Hebrews 7:11–14 the author shows that the Mosaic law[2] and Levitical priesthood (Ps. 110:4) were insufficient for bringing people to perfection (Heb. 7:18–19; 9:9; 10:1). How does the change in law and Jesus' role as High Priest in the line of Judah show that the Mosaic covenant is no longer in effect?

In the resurrection, Jesus seals his conquering of death and establishes his eternal priesthood (Heb. 5:6; 7:23–24). Because of Jesus' eternal priesthood, the former Levitical priesthood is set aside (7:18). What hope can believers draw from Jesus' finished work in relation to his heavenly priesthood (v. 19)?

In Hebrews 7:20–28 the author seals his argument for Jesus' superiority and divides it into three sections of thought:

1. Jesus' priesthood is guaranteed by the oath of God and is effective both for the present and for the future (7:20–22).
2. Jesus is able to save his people completely, and his people are able to draw near to God through him (vv. 23–25).
3. Jesus is the fitting High Priest, who offered himself for us and has been made perfect forever (vv. 26–28).

Walk through each section of thought and compare life under the old covenant and life under the new covenant, working out the implications as they pertain to salvation and everyday life. (See the chart in the *ESV Study Bible* on page 2372.)

3. Jesus, a Priest of a Better Covenant (8:1–13)

In Hebrews 8:1–6 the writer rehearses the main point of the letter thus far, namely, that believers have a superior High Priest who has offered the sacrifice of himself, is seated at the right hand of God, ministers in the heavenly sanctuary,[3] and thus mediates a better covenant. As we have already seen, Jesus is intimately familiar with both heaven and earth (4:14) and has completed his redemptive work. How does this truth strengthen a Christian's confidence in prayer life? How do these truths sustain faith in doubting or in difficult times?

The larger purpose of the Mosaic covenant was not to bring about perfection (8:7) but to inform people of God's holy law, reveal their sin, and establish a pattern of priesthood and sacrifice. Why then does God find fault with his people for not being able to uphold the first covenant, thus requiring a second covenant (8:8–13)?

In Hebrews 8:8–12, the author quotes Jeremiah 31:31–34 in its entirety. According to this Old Testament passage, what is the significant role of the

Messiah in establishing the new covenant? According to Jeremiah, what are
the implications of the work of this new covenant Messiah?

Read through the following three sections on *Gospel Glimpses, Whole-Bible
Connections*, and *Theological Soundings*. Then take time to reflect on the *Personal
Implications* these sections may have for your walk with the Lord.

▶ Gospel Glimpses

FORGIVENESS OF SIN. Believers in the Old Testament did receive forgiveness for their sins by casting themselves upon God and pleading for his mercy
through the sacrificial system. There were daily and yearly reminders of sin
built into the sanctuary and sacrificial system (Heb. 7:27; 8:3). But in the new
covenant Christ deals with sin once and for all, and God remembers our sins
no more (8:12). The blotting out of sin is essential to a relationship with God,
because if a person's sin is remembered by God, his holiness must take action
against that person. If the sins of the people are forgiven, it is because in his
grace God has determined to forgive them through Christ. Under the old sacrificial system there were reminders of sin; under Christ we must remind our-
selves that sin is dealt with once for all.

COVENANT MEDIATOR. A covenant is a binding agreement that provides a
basis for interaction between its parties. Jesus is identified as the Mediator of
this better new covenant between man and God (Heb. 7:20–22). In biblical and
legal terminology a mediator serves as arbiter between parties (see Job 9:33).
The intermediary ministry of the Levitical priests was only temporary and did
not grant entrance into the real heavenly presence of God. Rather, full entrance
into his eternal presence was achieved only with the life and redemptive
accomplishment of Jesus. Moreover, Jesus is greater than a mediator: he is also
a delegate invested with divine authority to guarantee the covenant. In this
sense, Jesus acted in the interest of both of the parties whom he represented.

NEW HEARTS. The new covenant described in Hebrews 8:8–12 involved
the writing of God's laws on people's hearts (not on tablets of stone, as in the
Mosaic covenant). In this way, the relationship between God and people will

be firmly established so that everyone within the covenant will know the Lord and his will in and from their hearts (vv. 10–11). As fallen human beings, our sinful hearts war within us against obedience to God's law. To be obedient, people need a new heart. In the new covenant, God's people's hearts are changed through the gospel and continue to change through the work of his Spirit.

Whole-Bible Connections

KING OF RIGHTEOUSNESS. Melchizedek is the first person in the Old Testament to be identified as a priest. Melchizedek reigned as the king of Salem, which, according to the Septuagint (a Greek translation of the Old Testament) can be identified as Jerusalem. Melchizedek's name literally means "king of righteousness." In the Old Testament, both righteousness and peace were related to messianic expectations (Isa. 9:6–7; Jer. 23:5; 33:15; Zech. 9:9–10). Melchizedek prefigured the Messiah, who would make righteousness and peace realities for his people. Jesus is the eternal King of righteousness and peace (Rom. 5:1; 14:17).

HEAVENLY SANCTUARY. The sanctuary (that is, the temple) served as the dwelling place of God in the midst of his people on earth; it was the place where God literally met with mankind. But the Old Testament sanctuary system was nothing but a shadowy copy of the heavenly reality (Heb. 8:5). From Eden to the tabernacle to the temple, we are granted a foreshadowing of the heavenly temple, where God's priests worship and minister in his presence. Jesus is the eternal High Priest who has brought full forgiveness of sins and who now ministers in the heavenly sanctuary on behalf of his people (8:1–3). One day, heaven and earth will meet again and form a heavenly sanctuary where God dwells with mankind (Revelation 21).

JEREMIAH'S HOPE. Jeremiah 31:31–34, which is quoted in Hebrews 8:8–12, is located in a section of Jeremiah referred to by many as the "book of hope." This Jeremiah passage offers hope to the exiled Israelites[4] that they will one day be restored to their homeland. In that day their mourning will be turned to gladness, and instead of sorrow their God will give them comfort and joy. In Christ, this hope finds its realization and ultimately its culmination (Rev. 21:1–5). Where the old covenant failed because of Israel's unbelief, the new covenant reality is secure under the perfect work of Christ.

Theological Soundings

GOD'S HOLINESS. God is absolutely holy, without sin, and uniquely above all of creation (Isa. 5:16; 6:1–8; Acts 3:14; Heb. 7:26; Rev. 4:8). Because of his holiness, God should be feared and obeyed. In order to draw near to God, one must be holy, innocent, and unstained by sin, since God is holy and separated from sinners. Thankfully, Jesus is the holy, pure, and blameless one who is able to cover sin and bring believers into the presence of God with his imputed righteousness upon them. Because of Christ's mediating work, we are able to draw near to the Holy One with confidence (Heb. 7:19, 25).

KNOWABILITY OF GOD. The knowledge of God in Christ is at the heart of the new covenant (Heb. 8:10–12). Intimate knowledge of God is something beyond what the old covenant offered. There was a sense in which the people of Israel knew their God, because he had revealed himself to them, which was in contrast to the other nations, who did not know him. However, in the new covenant community everyone can know God directly (v. 11). The Bible teaches that while we can have true and personal knowledge of God, we will never understand him exhaustively (Ps. 145:3; Job 26:14; Isa. 55:8–9; Rom. 11:33–34). However, in Christ God is most fully revealed (2 Cor. 4:4; Col. 1:15). The knowledge of God in Christ is the basis for obtaining eternal life (John 17:3).

NEW COVENANT. The image of a covenant is that of an agreement between God and his people where both parties are to remain faithful to their promises. Because of sin, the Israelites failed to obtain the blessings offered in the Mosaic covenant (Deut. 11:26–32). Therefore, it was necessary for God to establish a new covenant of grace through which his people could be saved. From Genesis 3, the story of Scripture is a story of God working out his plan of redemption. In Christ the new covenant is established and the blessings of God are graciously poured out on his redeemed people (Heb. 8:6–13; 13:20; Jer. 31:31–34; Ezek. 34:25–32).

▶ **Personal Implications**

Take time to reflect on the implications of Hebrews 7:1–8:13 for your own life today. Make notes below on the personal implications for your walk with the Lord of the (1) *Gospel Glimpses*, (2) *Whole-Bible Connections*, (3) *Theological Soundings*, and (4) this passage as a whole.

1. Gospel Glimpses

2. Whole-Bible Connections

---

3. Theological Soundings

---

4. Hebrews 7:1–8:13

> ### As You Finish This Unit . . .

Take a moment now to ask for the Lord's blessing and help as you continue in this study of Hebrews. And take a moment also to look back through this unit of study, to reflect on some things that the Lord may be teaching you—and perhaps to highlight or underline these to review again in the future.

Definitions

[1] **Covenant** – A binding agreement between two parties, typically involving a formal statement of their relationship, a list of stipulations and obligations for both parties, a list of witnesses to the agreement, and a list of curses for unfaithfulness and blessings for faithfulness to the agreement. The Old Testament is more properly understood as the old covenant, meaning the agreement established between God and his people prior to the coming of Jesus Christ and the establishment of the new covenant (New Testament).

[2] **Law** – When spelled with an initial capital letter in most Bible translations, "Law" refers to the first five books of the Bible (the Pentateuch). The Law contains numerous commands of God to his people, including the Ten Commandments and instructions regarding worship, sacrifice, and life in Israel. The New Testament often uses "the law" to refer to the entire body of precepts set forth in the books of the Law.

[3] **Sanctuary/Holy Place** – In the Bible, a place set aside as holy because of God's presence there. The inner sanctuary of the tabernacle (and later the temple) was called the Most Holy Place.

[4] **Israel** – Originally, another name given to Jacob (Gen. 32:28). Later applied to the nation formed by his descendants, then to the ten northern tribes of that nation, who rejected the anointed king and formed their own nation. In the New Testament, the name is applied to the church as the spiritual descendants of Abraham (Gal. 6:16).

WEEK 8: JESUS IS THE SUPERIOR SACRIFICE

Hebrews 9:1–10:18

The Place of the Passage

In Hebrews 9:1–10 the author describes the Old Testament tabernacle and worship patterns in order to lay the foundation for his discussion on the new covenant in chapter 10. The sacrifice of the greater High Priest Jesus is superior to the priestly worship of the Mosaic tabernacle (9:11–28). While the Mosaic priests continually offered sacrifices, Jesus offered himself as the perfect sacrifice once for all (10:1–18).

The Big Picture

Hebrews 9:1–10:18 proclaims Jesus as the new covenant High Priest whose perfect sacrifice of himself in the heavenly tabernacle brings forgiveness, salvation, a pure conscience, and direct access to God.

> ### Reflection and Discussion

Read through the complete passage for this study, Hebrews 9:1–10:18. After reading the entire passage, begin by rereading the portions listed and responding to the questions below. (For further background, see the *ESV Study Bible*, pages 2373–2378, available online at esv.org.)

1. The Earthly Holy Place (9:1–10)

In Hebrews 9:1–5 the author explains the Mosaic legislation governing worship and the proper way to approach a holy God. The earthly tabernacle had two sections—the Holy Place and the Most Holy Place—in which the provisions for worship were made through rituals and symbols pointing to God's past dealings with Israel and his continual presence with them (Exodus 25; 26:1–37; chs. 30; 37). How were these symbolic rituals and temporary provisions good news for the Israelites under the Mosaic covenant (Lev. 10:3; 16:20–25)?

The worship pattern involving the priests within the tabernacle is described in Hebrews 9:6–7. The priests went regularly into the Holy Place (the first section) to perform their duties and offer daily offerings (Ex. 25:30; 30:7–8; Lev. 24:4; Num. 28:7), while the high priest entered the Most Holy Place once a year to offer a sacrifice on the Day of Atonement[1] for all the sins of all the people (Leviticus 16). The Mosaic sacrificial system brought neither sanctification nor the fullness of God's peace to the worshiper (Heb. 9:8–10). How does the old covenant ritual heighten our sense of gratitude for Christ's work in establishing the new covenant?

----

2. Redemption through the Blood of Christ (9:11–28)

Christ entered the heavenly tabernacle once for all by the means of his own blood, securing eternal redemption for all of God's people (Heb. 9:12; see Ex. 20:24; 29:1–14; Lev. 16:6–19). According to Hebrews 9:13, the blood of goats and bulls cannot cleanse defiled sinners in their innermost being (Num. 19:1–22). Why does the blood of Christ accomplish what the blood of animals cannot (Heb. 9:14)?

Recalling the Mosaic covenant initiation ceremony (Ex. 24:3–8), the author shows that Christ initiates and mediates[2] the new covenant for his people by offering himself as a sacrifice[3] for their sin (Heb. 9:15; Rom. 8:30; 1 Thess. 5:24; 2 Tim. 1:9; 1 Pet. 5:10; 2 Pet. 1:10). In light of Exodus 40, how does the author connect the atoning blood sacrifice (Lev. 17:11) and the purpose of the blood of Christ (Heb. 9:16–22)?

Jesus entered the heavenly sanctuary, after which the earthly sanctuary was patterned (Heb. 9:11–14), and presented himself as an offering to God on the behalf of believers once for all (9:23–26a). This sacrifice had been needed since the fall of man, and it inaugurates the end of the ages, in which believers will await Christ's second coming (vv. 26b–28). How do reflection on Jesus' sacrifice and anticipation of his second coming motivate believers to love and obey him?

3. Christ's Sacrifice Once for All (10:1–18)

The repetition of the sacrifices under the Mosaic covenant not only convinced people of their sin, it also reminded them of their continual need for cleansing (Heb. 10:1–4). In quoting Psalm 40:6–8, the author of Hebrews points to God's true desire, what the sacrifices foreshadowed but could not seal for his people (Heb. 10:5–9). How do the life and work of Christ relate to the cry of David in this Psalm (v. 10)?

_____

_____

_____

_____

_____

Unlike the priests who made daily sacrifices, Christ offered himself as a sacrifice once for all, perfecting all who are being sanctified (Heb. 10:11–14). Christ's sacrifice not only affects the future sanctification of his people, it also affects the future of his enemies. How do the future implications of Christ's sacrifice motivate our holiness and our desire to proclaim the good news to others?

_____

_____

_____

_____

_____

By quoting from Jeremiah 31 in Hebrews 10:16–17 (compare 8:8–12), the author is reminding the reader that true believers will have God's laws internalized, and that God will remember their sins no more. Within the context of his argument in 10:1–18, explain what the author means when he says that no other offering is needed for sin (v. 18). What forgiveness and offering is he referring to?

_____

_____

_____

_____

_____

Read through the following three sections on *Gospel Glimpses*, *Whole-Bible Connections*, and *Theological Soundings*. Then take time to reflect on the *Personal Implications* these sections may have for your walk with the Lord.

Gospel Glimpses

POWER IN HIS BLOOD. Life is in the blood, and without the shedding of blood in a sacrifice there can be no forgiveness of sins (Lev. 17:11; Heb. 9:18). The shedding of human blood in the Old Testament was treated as a capital offense (Gen. 9:6). The shedding of animal blood was permitted in the Mosaic covenant in order to atone for the people's sin (Lev. 16:15). The animal sacrifices were repeated every year because of their inadequacy to purify the people (Heb. 10:4). Christ's personal sacrifice was sufficient once for all on behalf of his people, and his blood was adequate to obtain forgiveness of sin and establish a new covenant (Heb. 9:18; Mark 14:24).

FORGIVENESS OF GOD. The apostle John proclaimed that if we confess our sin, God is faithful and just to forgive us our sins and to cleanse us from all unrighteousness (1 John 1:9). In fact, because of the perfect work of Christ, the promise that God will remember our sins no more is secure (Jer. 31:34; Heb. 10:17). In Christ, our transgressions are removed as far as the east is from the west (Ps. 103:12). Therefore, God sees us as not cursed sinners but as cleansed saints—washed in the blood of his Son.

ONCE FOR ALL. In contrast to the repeated sacrifices of the Levitical priests, the sacrifice Christ made for the sins of mankind was made once for all (Heb. 9:25–26; 10:1–18). After Jesus' resurrection and ascension, he entered the presence of God in the Most Holy Place once for all, to be enthroned there in perpetuity (9:11–12). The salvation offered by Christ is perfect in every way, and eternal in its effect. Christ's once-for-all sacrifice is more than sufficient to save. In fact, there is no other name under heaven by which we can be saved (Acts 4:12).

Whole-Bible Connections

TABERNACLE. In the Old Testament, the tabernacle was the tent where God dwelled on earth and communed with his people as their divine King (Heb. 9:1–10; Ex. 33:9–11). The tabernacle was also referred to as the "tent of meeting" (Lev. 1:5). (The temple in Jerusalem later replaced it.) The primary function of the tabernacle was to represent God's holy presence on earth and to point to the heavenly tabernacle. The gospel of John announces Jesus as the

Word who took on flesh and dwelled (a verbal form of "tabernacle") among us (John 1:14). Through Christ, believers have direct access to God's presence (Heb. 4:16). One day Christ will return and consummate his kingdom; on that day God will dwell among his people forever (Rev. 21:3).

NEW COVENANT. The Mosaic covenant, established with Israel in the wilderness following the exodus, explains how they are to live as God's people (Ex. 19–20; see Deut. 11:26–32). In the Mosaic covenant God made certain requirements of his people and stipulated both blessings and curses depending on their faithfulness to the terms. The Israelites repeatedly failed to uphold their end. However, Jesus the true and greater Israelite fulfilled the covenant through his perfect life and once-for-all sacrifice on the cross (Heb. 9:1–10:18). Moreover, Christ mediates the covenant on behalf of God's people (9:15). The old covenant served as a shadow of the things to come in Christ (10:1). For this reason the new covenant is declared in Hebrews as new and better, because in Christ the old covenant finds its fulfillment (7:22; 8:6–13; 9:15; 12:24).

Theological Soundings

SANCTIFICATION AND JUSTIFICATION. In Hebrews 10:10 the author proclaims that believers have been sanctified once for all through the sacrifice of Jesus Christ. In Hebrews, sanctification is related to the Old Testament background of the ceremonial purity required to enter God's presence, by which one draws near to him (Heb. 9:13; 10:10; 13:12). The author of Hebrews's usage of "sanctification" is closely related in meaning to Paul's vocabulary of "justification" (Rom. 3:21–25; 5:1–9).

THE SECOND COMING OF CHRIST. Redemptive history has its goal and final working out of redemption in all its fullness in the coming kingdom of God. In the first coming of Christ, he inaugurated the kingdom of God through his life, crucifixion, and resurrection (Mark 1:15). In his second coming Jesus will consummate his kingdom (1 Thess. 4:15–17). The period in between his first and second coming is the "last days" (Heb. 1:2). Jesus "has appeared once for all at the end of the ages to put away sin by the sacrifice of himself" (9:26).

Personal Implications

Take time to reflect on the implications of Hebrews 9:1–10:18 for your own life today. Make notes below on the personal implications for your walk with the Lord of the (1) *Gospel Glimpses*, (2) *Whole-Bible Connections*, (3) *Theological Soundings*, and (4) this passage as a whole.

1. Gospel Glimpses

2. Whole-Bible Connections

3. Theological Soundings

4. Hebrews 9:1–10:18

▶ **As You Finish This Unit . . .**

Take a moment now to ask for the Lord's blessing and help as you continue in this study of Hebrews. And take a moment also to look back through this unit of study, to reflect on some things that the Lord may be teaching you—and perhaps to highlight or underline these to review again in the future.

Definitions

[1] **Day of Atonement** – The holiest day in the Israelite calendar, when atonement was made for all the sins of Israel during the past year (Leviticus 16). It occurred on the tenth day of the seventh month (September/October), on which all Israel was to fast and do no work. Only on that day each year could someone—the high priest—enter the Most Holy Place of the tabernacle (later, the temple) and offer the necessary sacrifices. A "scapegoat" would also be sent into the wilderness as a sign of Israel's sins being carried away.

[2] **Mediator** – One who intercedes between parties to resolve a conflict or achieve a goal. Jesus is the Mediator between God and rebellious humanity (1 Tim. 2:5; compare Heb. 9:15; 12:24).

[3] **Sacrifice** – An offering to God, often to achieve forgiveness of sin. The Law of Moses gave detailed instructions regarding various kinds of sacrifices. By his death on the cross, Jesus gave himself as a sacrifice to atone for the sins of believers (Eph. 5:2; Heb. 10:12). Believers are to offer their bodies as living sacrifices to God (Rom. 12:1).

WEEK 9: THE CALL TO FAITH

Hebrews 10:19–11:40

▲

The Place of the Passage

Knowing the truth of Christ's person and work, readers are exhorted to draw near to God. In this passage the readers receive their fourth warning, namely, against shrinking back from faith (Heb. 10:19–39). In 11:1–40, faith is described as consisting of persevering hope in the promises of God, and is illustrated by the lives and actions of many Old Testament "heroes." It is this type of persevering faith that results in salvation on the last day. Accordingly, judgment awaits those who willfully reject the faith.

The Big Picture

Hebrews 10:19–11:40 shows the sufficiency of Jesus' work in making a way to God, and calls the reader to imitate the persevering faith of the Old Testament saints as they await final consummation in Christ.

> ## Reflection and Discussion

Read through the complete passage for this study, Hebrews 10:19–11:40. After reading the entire passage, begin by rereading the portions listed and responding to the questions below. (For further background, see the *ESV Study Bible*, pages 2378–2382, available online at esv.org.)

1. Exhortation to Draw Near (10:19–25)

Through Christ, access into the holy places has been secured so that believers can draw near to God with confidence (Heb. 10:19–22). The author employs the imagery of the curtain being opened in order to grant access to God (v. 20). What is this imagery intended to communicate to the reader (Heb. 9:3; Exodus 26; 36; Matt. 27:51)?

In Hebrews 10:22–24 the author exhorts his readers toward the three cardinal Christian virtues of faith, hope, and love (1 Cor. 13:13; 1 Thess. 1:3; 5:8). In what ways are each of these virtues tied to the work of Jesus Christ the great High Priest?

According to the author, Christian perseverance is a community endeavor (Heb. 10:25). By what means, and for what purpose, does the author argue for community-encouraged perseverance?

2. Warning Four: Against Shrinking Back (10:26–39)

By willfully sinning and refusing to repent after receiving knowledge of the true gospel, one turns one's back on the only means of forgiveness (Heb. 10:26–27). In these cases, only the fearful expectation of judgment awaits. Why does the author relate this warning to the Old Testament cases of people setting aside the Mosaic law (vv. 28–29; Lev. 24:13–16; Deut. 17:2–7)?

By spurning the Son of God, profaning the blood of the covenant, and outraging the Spirit of grace, those who have rejected the knowledge of truth have placed themselves in the hands of the living God and face judgment (Heb. 10:29–31; Deut. 32:35–36). In what ways is this passage intended to reveal superficial faith or reinforce perseverance in the saints?

After sternly warning his audience, the author encourages them with previous evidence concerning their faith (Heb. 10:32–34). They are then exhorted to endure with confidence in doing the will of God (10:35–36). What does the citation of Habakkuk 2:3–4 in Hebrews 10:37–38 teach us about the relationship between righteousness and faith? In verse 39, from where does the author draw his confidence in the believers to whom he is writing?

3. By Faith (11:1–40)

Oftentimes, faith is related to the unseen realities of God. Considering that the author uses the words "assurance" and "conviction" regarding the promises of God, how does this inform our definition of biblical faith (Heb. 11:1–3)?

In Hebrews 11:4–40, we learn that faith consists of persistent hope in God's promises, and that such persevering faith leads to salvation on the last day (10:39). Throughout this chapter the author lists Old Testament saints who serve as models of persevering faith in life and deed. In what way does the author intend to motivate faith and perseverance from each story mentioned in Hebrews 11? (Many of these reference the section titled, "History of Salvation in the Old Testament," in the ESV *Study Bible*, pages 2635–2661.)

- Abel (11:4; Genesis 4)
- Enoch (11:5; Gen. 5:18–24)
- Noah (11:7; Gen. 5:29–10:32)
- Abraham (11:8–19; Genesis 12–25)
- Sarah (11:11; Genesis 12–23; Isa. 51:2)
- Isaac (11:17–20; Genesis 17–35)
- Jacob (11:21; Genesis 25–50)
- Joseph (11:21–22; Genesis 37–50)
- Moses (11:23–28; Ex. 2:10 and throughout the Pentateuch)
- Rahab (11:31; Joshua 2; 6:17–25)
- Gideon (11:32; Judges 6–8)

- Barak (11:32; Judges 4–5)
- Samson (11:32; Judges 13–16)
- Jephthah (11:32; Judges 11–12; 1 Sam. 12:11)
- David (11:32; Ruth 4; 1–2 Samuel)
- Samuel (11:32; 1 Samuel; 1 Chron. 6; 9; 11; 26; 2 Chron. 35:18)

Most of the people mentioned in Hebrews 11 experienced only preliminary glimpses of what was promised to them by God and were anticipating a greater future reality (11:39–40). According to 11:40, what is the greater reality that they, and we, await?

Read through the following three sections on *Gospel Glimpses*, *Whole-Bible Connections*, and *Theological Soundings*. Then take time to reflect on the *Personal Implications* these sections may have for your walk with the Lord.

▶ Gospel Glimpses

CONSUMMATION. "The Day" refers to the second coming of Christ. On that "Day" Christ will return, judge, and consummate the kingdom of God on earth (Heb. 9:28; 10:25, 27, 37; see Amos 5:18–20; 2 Tim. 1:12). In consummating his kingdom, Jesus will not only finally rescue all sinners but will also restore creation, bringing heaven and earth together (Rom. 8:21; 2 Pet. 3:7–13; Rev. 21:1–22:6). The promise of God's kingdom finally being consummated provides believers the hope needed to hold fast, and can be a basis for their mutual encouragement through trials (Heb. 10:23–25).

APOSTASY. By God's grace, those in the church are continually warned of the danger of falling into apostasy (Heb. 6:4–8; 10:26–31). All people face judgment because of sin (9:27–28), and apart from Jesus' sacrifice all his adversaries face God's judgment. The warning verses of Hebrews call Christians to faith, obedience, and perseverance.

ASSURANCE OF FAITH IN WORKS. The warning passages in Hebrews have often raised doubts about the salvation of the original audience, and even about assurance of salvation in general. True assurance of salvation is affirmed in other passages of the Bible (John 6:39–40, 44; Romans 5; 8:29–30). As for the original audience, according to Hebrews 6:10 they have a track record of Christian service, which is confirmed in 10:32–34 and 13:1–3. The book of Hebrews contains a strong emphasis on true conversion being marked by a godly diligence that perseveres, which in turn provides assurance that God's Spirit is at work (Matt. 7:15–17). The list of Old Testament saints in Hebrews 11:1–40 illustrates the relationship between faith and works. Because of their faith in God's Word, these saints were trusted with God's Word, were patiently awaiting the fulfillment of God's Word, and were obedient to God's Word by working out their faith (See Phil. 2:12–13). Gospel faith is demonstrated and manifested in good works to the glory of God.

▶ Whole-Bible Connections

THE HOLY PLACE. The opening chapters of Genesis present the garden of Eden as a holy place, a divine sanctuary where God dwells with man (Gen. 3:8). After the fall, the tabernacle and temple function in a way similar to the garden, being the holy place where God dwells (Lev. 26:12; Deut. 23:14; 2 Sam. 7:6–7). However, because of sin God cannot dwell with man in the same way as he did in the garden. But because of the work of Christ, believers are given access to God and encouraged to draw near to him in the heavenly holy places. Throughout redemptive history we witness the progression from a holy garden to a holy city—a place where a holy God will dwell with his people once again (Rev. 21:1–3).

STRANGERS AND EXILES. In the Bible, an "exile" is one who has been banished from his or her native place or is wandering in foreign regions. The imagery originated when the human race was exiled from the garden of Eden (Gen. 3:24). Further notable instances of exile include Israel's wandering in the wilderness following the exodus,[1] and their later being driven from their land by Assyria (northern kingdom; 2 Kings 17) and Babylon (southern kingdom; 2 Kings 25). Similarly, Hebrews 11 refers to believers as strangers and exiles on earth seeking a better country (11:13, 16). In Hebrews 2 Christ is referred to as the founder and leader of God's people, which harkens to his role in delivering his people to the greater Promised Land of heaven.

▶ Theological Soundings

CREATION FROM NOTHING. According to the Bible, before God began to create the universe, nothing existed except him (Ps. 90:2; Rom. 4:17). Without using any preexisting material, God spoke the universe and everything in it into existence (Ps. 33:9; Heb. 11:3). Moreover, all things were made through him and for him (Col. 1:16).

EXTENT OF THE ATONEMENT. Christ's life and work earned our salvation. He atoned for our sin. However, if someone continues in sin after receiving knowledge of the truth, there no longer remains a sacrifice for sins (Heb. 10:26). It is not that Christ's sacrifice no longer exists, but it is not applied to the one who rejects him. Sacrifice for sin is available and applied to those who believe (1 Tim. 2:6; 1 John 2:2), and they are Christ's people (Heb. 2:9–13; 8:11).

WORSHIP. Under the Mosaic covenant, God's people could draw near to him in only a limited way, through temple ceremonies. Even then, most of the people of Israel remained in the courtyard, outside the temple (Heb. 9:1–7). In the new covenant, worshipers enjoy the presence of God himself, and in worship they enter before his throne (10:19, 22). Through Christ, God makes true worship real for his children (12:28; 13:15–16).

Personal Implications

Take time to reflect on the implications of Hebrews 10:19–11:40 for your own life today. Make notes below on the personal implications for your walk with the Lord of the (1) *Gospel Glimpses*, (2) *Whole-Bible Connections*, (3) *Theological Soundings*, and (4) this passage as a whole.

1. Gospel Glimpses

2. Whole-Bible Connections

3. Theological Soundings

4. Hebrews 10:19–11:40

> ## As You Finish This Unit . . .

Take a moment now to ask for the Lord's blessing and help as you continue in this study of Hebrews. And take a moment also to look back through this unit of study, to reflect on some things that the Lord may be teaching you—and perhaps to highlight or underline these to review again in the future.

Definitions

[1] **Exodus** – The departure of the people of Israel from Egypt and their journey to Mount Sinai under Moses' leadership (Exodus 1–19; Numbers 33). The exodus demonstrated God's power and providence for his people, who had been enslaved by the Egyptians. The annual festival of Passover[2] commemorates God's final plague upon the Egyptians, resulting in Israel's release from Egypt.

[2] **Passover** – An annual Israelite festival commemorating God's final plague on the Egyptians, which led to the exodus. In this final plague, the Lord "passed over" the houses of those who spread the blood of a lamb on the doorposts of their homes (Exodus 12). But all who did not obey this command suffered the death of their firstborn.

WEEK 10: THE CALL TO ENDURANCE

Hebrews 12:1–29

▲

The Place of the Passage

Given the past examples of persevering faith (Hebrews 11), including Jesus' own endurance of the cross[1] (12:1–2), Christians are to endure in the faith, knowing that God's discipline is for their good (12:3–11). In this fifth and final warning, the readers are cautioned against rejecting God's grace and placing themselves under his judgment (vv. 12–17, 25). God's kingdom cannot be shaken, and one must respond in faithful worship (vv. 18–29).

The Big Picture

Hebrews 12:1–29 reminds the readers that Jesus is the founder and perfecter of the faith, and that it is in response to Christ's endurance of the cross that they are to persevere in faith.

> ### Reflection and Discussion

Read through the complete passage for this study, Hebrews 12:1–29. After reading the entire passage, begin by rereading the portions listed and responding to the questions below. (For further background, see the *ESV Study Bible*, pages 2382–2384, available online at esv.org.)

1. Jesus, Founder and Perfecter of Our Faith (12:1–2)

The Old Testament "heroes" listed in Hebrews 11 witnessed to their faith through word and deed. As we look back at their faithful example, like spectators in an arena, how are we encouraged to run with endurance the race set before us (12:1; 1 Cor. 9:24–27; 2 Tim. 4:7–8)?

After giving past examples of faith, the author reminds readers that it is Jesus' perfecting of their faith that leads to perfection in his people (Heb. 12:2). Because of the future reward set before him, Jesus endured the greatest suffering in history in consuming God's wrath against sin on the cross (Matt. 27:27–50). How does Jesus' perfect endurance not only solidify our future hope but also encourage our perseverance as we wait?

2. Do Not Grow Weary (12:3–17)

Considering Jesus' endurance in light of the hostility shown him, the readers are urged not to grow weary or fainthearted (Heb. 12:3). The struggle against sin will always be the greatest hostility believers face in this life. In verses 5b–6, how does the author use Proverbs 3:11–12 to instruct his readers concerning God's tests and discipline? Furthermore, what is the intended outcome of the heavenly Father's discipline (Heb. 12:7–11)?

Using poetic language to inspire the readers to continue to the end (Heb. 12:12–13), the author encourages them to pursue peace with others and holiness in themselves in response to Christ's work. Why is the pursuit of peace so important within the Christian community (Mark 9:50; Rom. 12:18–21; 14:19; 2 Cor. 13:11)? What motivates Christ's church in maintaining peace and watching over one another (Heb. 12:14–15)?

In Hebrews 12:16–17, the priority of holiness and sexual purity is contrasted with the example of Esau, who because of his false priorities is deemed unholy (Gen. 25:33–34; 26:34–35; 28:6–8). Even though Esau desired the blessing, even in tears, he showed no true repentance for his actions. In what ways is it possible to desire the blessings of repentance without truly being broken over sin?

3. A Kingdom That Cannot Be Shaken (12:18–24)

The author uses Israel's experience at Mount Sinai (Heb. 12:18–21) as an example of the fear that loomed over God's people under the Mosaic covenant

(Ex. 19:12–25; 20:18–21; Deut. 18:16). In Deuteronomy 9:19, which is quoted in this passage, Moses expresses fear that God would destroy Israel in their idolatry. In what ways is the threat of idolatry still as dangerous today, even for the church?

While the Israelites trembled in fear at Mount Sinai, new covenant believers can access the new heavenly Zion before the living God with joy and confidence because of Christ's work (12:22–24). What is the picture painted here of the new heavenly Zion/Jerusalem (see Isa. 62:6–12)? What aspects of this imagery provoke longing within you?

4. Warning Five: Against Refusing the Speaker (12:25–29)

In light of the new covenant and Jesus' eternal reign in heaven,[2] the readers are beckoned to respond in faith before Christ returns again to judge and it is too late (Heb. 12:25–27). As we have already seen, through Christ we are able to approach God in confidence, but how does this passage instruct us in the proper manner of worship (12:28–29)?

Read through the following three sections on *Gospel Glimpses*, *Whole-Bible Connections*, and *Theological Soundings*. Then take time to reflect on the *Personal Implications* these sections may have for your walk with the Lord.

> ## Gospel Glimpses

FOUNDER AND PERFECTER. Jesus is the founder and perfecter of our faith (Heb. 12:2). Jesus is the champion of salvation who lives in perfect obedience and complete faith for the sake of his people. Through his perfect atoning sacrifice he secures our salvation, and his perfection leads to the perfection of his people, which will be realized on the last day (see 11:39–40). First to last, God's people are completely and utterly reliant on Jesus for salvation and sanctification.

HOLINESS. God's people are called to be "set apart" or holy (Lev. 18:2–4; 1 Pet. 1:15–16). Holiness includes full ethical purity and freedom from sin. Because God is holy, without holiness no one will see him (Heb. 12:14). Thankfully, Christians are set apart as holy through the once-for-all sacrifice of Christ on the cross (10:14). In response to God's grace, Christians are called to persevere in holiness as worship. Moreover, God will discipline his children in order that we might share in his holiness (12:10).

> ## Whole-Bible Connections

RIGHT HAND OF GOD. Several times in the book of Hebrews the author notes that Jesus is seated at the right hand of God (1:3, 13; 8:1; 10:12; 12:2). In the Old Testament, the "right hand" is a reference to power and honor, and is a position occupied at the right side of a human king (1 Kings 2:19; Ps. 45:9). In the poetic language of the Bible, the hand of God, and especially the right hand, is symbolic of a place of salvation, refuge, protection, and pleasure (Ps. 16:11; 17:7; 48:10; 80:17; 89:13; 110:1; 118:16). King Jesus sits at God's right hand, where he intercedes for believers (Rom. 8:34; Heb. 8:1) and exercises authority and power over all things (1 Pet. 3:22).

SINAI TO NEW ZION. The terrors of Mount Sinai, where the Israelites received the Ten Commandments from God, were real and palpable (Ex. 20:18–21; Heb. 12:18–21). The Lord's awesome presence brought with it fire and cloud, thunder and lightning (Ex. 19:16–19; see Deut. 9:19). God descended on Sinai to declare his holy law, and Moses feared that God would destroy his people for their unholy worship of idols—a problem by which God's sinful people would perpetually be ensnared. However, Christ came to live the perfect, sinless life

God's people could not live, and offered himself to be destroyed for their sin. Through Christ, God's people are granted access to the new heavenly Zion, to worship God in reverence and awe without the fear of being destroyed (Heb. 12:22–28).

KINGDOM. In many ways, the garden of Eden functioned as a prototype of God's kingdom. Adam and Eve were to serve as vice regents and exercise dominion over Eden as God's kingdom (Gen. 1:26–28). However, when Adam and Eve attempted to dethrone God, the Edenic kingdom was shaken, paradise was lost, and the entire human race was exiled (Genesis 3). Later in the biblical narrative, God's people desired a king because of their lack of faith (1 Samuel 8). Even the greatest of the Israelite kings failed to live up to God's ideal (1 Samuel 31; 2 Samuel 11–12; 1 Kings 11:1–6). However, Jesus came as the true and perfect king to reign with righteousness and justice forever (Heb. 12:22–24, 28). Christ inaugurated the kingdom of God[3] in his first coming and will consummate his kingdom at his second coming (Luke 17:20–22; Rev. 1:9; 11:15). Jesus is the second Adam and eternal King in the kingdom that cannot be shaken, the eternal Eden paradise of God.

Theological Soundings

THE LIVING GOD. In Hebrews we learn that God is not a vague cosmic concept or simply the opiate of the masses. Several times in Hebrews he is referred to as the living God (Heb. 3:12; 10:31; 12:22; see Matt. 16:16; Acts 14:15; Rom. 9:26; Rev. 7:2). The God of the Bible is both an infinite and a personal being.

DISCIPLINE OF GOD. When Christians sin, their legal standing before God remains unchanged (Rom. 6:23; 8:1; 1 Cor. 15:3), but their fellowship with God is disrupted, their lives are damaged, and God's Spirit is grieved (John 15:4; Rom. 6:16; Eph. 4:30). And all Christians sin (1 John 1:8). The author of Hebrews reminds us that God disciplines those he loves as a father lovingly disciplines his child (Heb. 12:6; Prov. 3:11–12; 1 John 3:2). God's discipline is for our good, that we may share in his holiness (Heb. 12:10). Therefore, we are reminded by Jesus to confess sin daily, knowing that God will forgive us (Matt. 6:12). Not only does God discipline us for our good, but it is often God who lovingly brings us to repentance (Rom. 2:4).

Personal Implications

Take time to reflect on the implications of Hebrews 12:1–29 for your own life today. Make notes below on the personal implications for your walk with the Lord of the (1) *Gospel Glimpses*, (2) *Whole-Bible Connections*, (3) *Theological Soundings*, and (4) this passage as a whole.

1. Gospel Glimpses

2. Whole-Bible Connections

3. Theological Soundings

4. Hebrews 12:1–29

As You Finish This Unit . . .

Take a moment now to ask for the Lord's blessing and help as you continue in this study of Hebrews. And take a moment also to look back through this unit of study, to reflect on some things that the Lord may be teaching you—and perhaps to highlight or underline these to review again in the future.

Definitions

[1] **Cross** – Crucifixion was a means of execution in which the person was fastened, by ropes or nails, to a crossbeam that was then raised and attached to a vertical beam, forming a cross (the root meaning of "crucifixion"). The process was designed to maximize pain and humiliation, and to serve as a deterrent for other potential offenders. Jesus suffered this form of execution (Matt. 27:32–56), not for any offense he had committed (Heb. 4:15) but as the atoning sacrifice for all who would believe in him (John 3:16).

[2] **Heaven** – The sky, or the abode of God (Matt. 6:9), which is commonly regarded as being above the earth and sky. As the abode of God, heaven is also the place where believers live in God's presence after death (1 Thess. 4:16–17).

[3] **Kingdom of God** – The sovereign rule of God. At the present time, the fallen, sinful world does not belong to the kingdom of God, since it does not submit to God's rule. Instead, God's kingdom can be found in heaven and among his people on earth (Matt. 6:9–10; Luke 17:20–21). After Christ returns, however, the kingdoms of the world will become the kingdom of God (Rev. 11:15). Then all people will, either willingly or regretfully, acknowledge his sovereignty (Phil. 2:9–11). Even the natural world will be transformed to operate in perfect harmony with God (Rom. 8:19–23).

WEEK 11: FINAL EXHORTATIONS

Hebrews 13:1–25

▲

As the letter comes to a close, the author exhorts[1] the community concerning specific points of application, covers them in a blessing, and issues final greetings (Heb. 13:1–25). The moral exhortations in this passage focus on hospitality, marriage, money, church leadership, and guarding against heresy.[2] The church is called to leave behind love of this world and embrace the reproach of Christ. The author closes with confidence, knowing that God himself will equip the readers to do his will.

The Big Picture

Hebrews 13:1–25 depicts Jesus Christ as the sacrifice slaughtered outside the camp so that we could be presented as sanctified and could worship in the presence of God.

> ### Reflection and Discussion

Read through the complete passage for this study, Hebrews 13:1–25. After reading the entire passage, begin by rereading the portions listed and responding to the questions below. (For further background, see the *ESV Study Bible*, pages 2385–2386, available online at esv.org.)

1. Sacrifices Pleasing to God (13:1–19)

Not only are relationships within the church marked by love (v. 1), but also the church is to be marked by hospitality to strangers (v. 2; Rom. 12:13; 1 Tim. 3:2; Titus 1:8). In ancient times, travel was difficult and inns were not only dangerous but were also notorious for immorality. Hebrews 13:2 recalls Abraham's hospitality toward his mysterious visitors in Genesis 18–19. Based on that narrative, for what reasons should believers practice hospitality?

In Hebrews 13:3, the writer reminds believers to remember those who are in prison, and to treat them as if they were in prison along with them. Prisoners relied on those outside to sustain their lives. In many ways this is a specific application of Matthew 7:12 in calling the church to respond to the real needs of those around them. Beyond mere Christian charity and hospitality, what else should motivate us to care for those in need (Matt. 25:35–36)?

Within the Christian community, marriage is to be held in honor. It is clear from Hebrews 13:4 that God will judge anyone who is sexually immoral or adulterous. In light of the earlier warning passages, continual sexual sin without repentance is an indication that one is not a true believer. Since this warning is addressed to the church, what type of judgment is the author referring to (Rom. 8:1; Heb. 12:5–11)?

Christians are also to be marked by contentment with God's provision (Heb. 13:5–6; Deut. 31:6, 8; Josh 1:15). The love of money is a strong indicator that one is not content with God in many areas of life. How does Psalm 118:6, which is quoted in Hebrews 13:6, remind us of the security of God's provision?

Readers are encouraged to listen to their leaders, who are charged with shepherding them through preaching and teaching God's Word, and who are themselves under the authority of the Good Shepherd Jesus Christ (Heb. 13:7–8, 17). The author warns them of heresy; the central concern here appears to be teachings about foods (vv. 9–11). What are the dangers of diverse and strange doctrines that depart from Jesus?

In Hebrews 13:10–12, Jesus' sacrifice is contrasted with the sin offering on the Day of Atonement under the Mosaic covenant (Lev. 16:27). Unlike the priests in the Old Testament, who could not partake of the sacrifice (Heb. 13:10), believers are to partake in the sacrifice of Christ for spiritual nourishment. By Jesus' death "outside the camp" (vv. 11–12; see John 19:17–20) and by his blood within the Most Holy Place, believers are granted access to God. What are the benefits of these truths for the Christian life?

Through metaphor, the author encourages his readers to leave behind their love for this world and embrace the reproach of Christ (Heb. 13:13). How does the author's declaration of this world's temporary nature (v. 14) strengthen his words of encouragement (v. 13)?

The proper response to Christ's work is worship. Therefore, the author calls us to offer a sacrifice of praise not only with our lips but also with our actions toward others (Heb. 13:15–16). Why does the author mention that such things are pleasing to God?

At the end of his letter the author mentions several requests and desires (Heb. 13:18–19). As Christians, what are some practical ways that we too can pursue a "clear conscience" regarding our service, and a desire to "act honorably" toward all?

---

2. Benediction and Final Greetings (13:20–25)

In his benediction[3] the author offers a doxological blessing to his readers (Heb. 13:20–21) and closes the letter with some final greetings (vv. 22–25). How does his benediction summarize his letter? Which particular aspect of this benediction brings you the most hope, joy, or comfort?

Read through the following three sections on *Gospel Glimpses, Whole-Bible Connections*, and *Theological Soundings*. Then take time to reflect on the *Personal Implications* these sections may have for your walk with the Lord.

Gospel Glimpses

REPROACH OF CHRIST. Christ truly suffered on behalf of God's people (Heb. 2:18; 5:8; 13:12). Moses also suffered on behalf of the people of God, and is said to have borne Christ's reproach (11:26). In this way, Moses serves as an example for believers to bear such reproach (10:33; 13:13). Jesus endured the suffering of the cross for the joy set before him (12:2). Believers are called to do likewise, namely, emulate Jesus' response to suffering because of the joy that lies ahead, secured for them in the gospel.

RESURRECTION OF CHRIST. After Jesus was crucified and buried, God "brought" him from the dead three days later (Heb. 13:20; see also 5:7; 7:16; Matthew 28). The resurrection of Christ is the central doctrine of the Christian faith (1 Cor. 15:14, 17). Jesus' resurrection not only proved his defeat of sin and death; it also secured salvation and began the era of new creation (1 Cor. 15:20–23; 2 Cor. 5:17; Col. 1:15–20). Those who trust in Christ will also be resurrected, on the last day (Rom. 6:5; 1 Pet. 1:3). Resurrection gives Christians the hope that one day God will make all things new.

THE GOOD SHEPHERD. The imagery of sheep, shepherd, and sheepfold was a central part of Israel's heritage (Psalm 23). Jesus identified himself as the good shepherd (John 10:1–21; see Zech. 13:7–9) who gives his life for his sheep (see 1 Sam. 17:34–37; Isa. 40:11). According to Psalm 23:4, a good shepherd not only protects his sheep (rod), but also provides comforts (staff). The author of Hebrews ends his exhortatory letter with a reminder that the Great Shepherd Jesus Christ will give the readers all they need, to do what is pleasing in God's sight (Heb. 13:20–21; see 1 Pet. 2:25; 5:4).

► Whole-Bible Connections

OUTSIDE THE GATE/CAMP. Unlike other Old Testament offerings, the tabernacle priests could not partake of the sin offering from the Day of Atonement since it was considered unclean,[4] and thus was burned outside the camp (Heb. 13:11; Lev. 16:27). Jesus was crucified "outside the gate," referring to Calvary, which was outside the gates of Jerusalem (Matt. 27:22; Mark 15:21–22). Jesus went outside the gate, to the place of uncleanliness, in order to wash his people clean and make them holy (Heb. 2:11; 10:10, 14). In his perfect sacrifice, Jesus' blood provides atonement for sin (9:11–14).

SACRIFICES PLEASING TO GOD. The Psalmists often speak of sacrifices of praise (Ps. 50:14, 23; 107:22; 116:17). In these Psalms, a sacrifice of praise refers to a sacrificial animal offered to God after divine deliverance. In Hebrews 13:15–16, sacrifices of praise refer to verbal acclaim and good deeds done to the glory of God (see 12:28–29). The once-for-all sacrifice of Christ has brought eternal deliverance from sin and death, and the proper response to God's grace is a life of worship in word and deed (Rom. 12:1)

► Theological Soundings

IMMUTABILITY OF GOD. God is unchanging in his promises and purposes and can always be trusted (Num. 23:19; Ps. 33:11; Isa. 46:9–11; Rom. 11:29). God is faithful and always truthful (2 Sam. 7:28; Ps. 141:6). In Hebrews 6:18 the author writes that it is impossible for God to lie; therefore God can always be taken at his word. The essence of the truthfulness of Scripture rests in the immutability of God and the trustworthiness of his Word. Similarly, Jesus Christ is trustworthy because he is the same yesterday, today, and forever (13:8).

CHURCH LEADERSHIP. One of the primary functions of an elder in the New Testament is that of governing the church (1 Tim. 5:17; 1 Pet. 5:2–5). In Hebrews 13:17 the author urges the readers to obey their elders, who will give an account for how they "are keeping watch over your souls" (v. 17; compare Acts 20:28).

▶ **Personal Implications**

Take time to reflect on the implications of Hebrews 13:1–25 for your own life today. Make notes below on the personal implications for your walk with the Lord of the (1) *Gospel Glimpses*, (2) *Whole-Bible Connections*, (3) *Theological Soundings*, and (4) this passage as a whole.

1. Gospel Glimpses

2. Whole-Bible Connections

3. Theological Soundings

4. Hebrews 13:1–25

> ## As You Finish This Unit . . .

Take a moment now to ask for the Lord's blessing and help as you continue in this study of Hebrews. And take a moment also to look back through this unit of study, to reflect on some things that the Lord may be teaching you—and perhaps to highlight or underline these to review again in the future.

Definitions

[1] **Exhortation** – A message encouraging someone to follow a particular course of action or to submit to a different way of thinking.

[2] **Heresy** – Any teaching incompatible with Christian orthodoxy.

[3] **Benediction** – A prayer for God's blessing at the end of a letter or a worship service. Many New Testament letters include a benediction.

[4] **Clean/unclean** – The ceremonial, spiritual, or moral state of a person or object, affected by a variety of factors. The terms are primarily related to the concept of holiness and have little to do with actual physical cleanliness. The Mosaic law declared certain foods and animals unclean, and a person became unclean if he or she came in contact with certain substances or objects, such as a dead body. Jesus declared all foods clean (Mark 7:19), and Peter's vision in Acts 10 shows that no person is ceremonially unclean simply because he or she is a Gentile.

Week 12: Summary and Conclusion

As we draw this study of Hebrews to a close, we begin by looking at the big picture of Hebrews as a whole. We will then review some questions for reflection in light of our study through the book of Hebrews, with a final reflection on Gospel Glimpses, Whole-Bible Connections, and Theological Soundings, all with a view of appreciating Hebrews in its entirety.

The Big Picture of Hebrews

Over the course of our studies in Hebrews we have come to see the supremacy of Jesus Christ over all things. The central motif of Hebrews is "Jesus Christ is better." For the author of Hebrews, the glory of God as revealed in Jesus Christ is the gravitational center of his exhortation. Using a powerful theological argument for the superiority of Christ, the author encourages readers to persevere in the faith and warns them against falling away. Throughout the book, by the author's encouraging words, firm warnings, and contrasting examples, readers are called to respond to Christ in worship.

We have seen that, among other things, Jesus is superior to angelic beings (Heb. 1:5–2:8), superior to Moses (3:1–4:13), the superior High Priest (4:14–5:10; 7:1–8:13), and the superior sacrifice (9:1–10:18). The readers are warned against neglecting salvation (2:1–4), forfeiting their rest in God (4:1–13), apostasy (5:11–6:20), shrinking back from their faith (10:26–39), and of refusing God's message and his messenger (12:25–29). In light of all these things, the reader is called to faith and endurance (10:19–12:29).

Read through the following three sections on *Gospel Glimpses, Whole-Bible Connections*, and *Theological Soundings*. Then take time to reflect on the *Personal Implications* these sections may have for your walk with the Lord.

▶ Gospel Glimpses

Throughout the book of Hebrews we have seen the grace of God in the gospel of Jesus Christ. Jesus is shown as the eternal Son, King, High Priest, and perfect sacrifice, and as the author and perfecter of our faith. The author of Hebrews has shown us how the institutions, rituals, and offices of the Old Testament were mere shadows of Jesus, who is the substance. Throughout, we are reminded of the sufficiency, perfection, and finality of Jesus' life and work in accomplishing and sustaining our salvation.

How has your understanding of the gospel changed during the course of this study?

Are there any particular images, metaphors, allusions, analogies, or typological connections between Jesus and the Old Testament that have brought the gospel home to you in a new way?

As you've studied Hebrews, how has the explanation of the old covenant and Mosaic law deepened your understanding and appreciation of the new covenant of grace in Jesus Christ?

> ## Whole-Bible Connections

Hebrews is rich in quotations from the Old Testament, along with many allusions and references. With the Old Testament background in mind, the author argues that God's glory and redemptive plan are finally and most clearly revealed in Jesus Christ. The superiority of Jesus Christ is demonstrated in that he is greater than any angel, priest, or old covenant institution. Christ is the complete atoning sacrifice and final priest. In him we see the fulfillment of all the Old Testament hopes and promises, ushering in the long-awaited new covenant age.

How has your understanding of the Old Testament been deepened through your study of Hebrews?

What are some connections between the Old Testament and Christ that you hadn't noticed before?

How has your understanding of the unity of the Bible been clarified through this study in Hebrews?

How would you argue for the superiority of Jesus Christ from the following Old Testament themes, offices, and persons?

- The angels
- The Mosaic law
- The Old Testament high priest
- The old covenant sacrifices

Theological Soundings

Hebrews contributes much to our understanding of our Trinitarian God and the core Christian doctrines. Doctrines that are reinforced in Hebrews include our understanding of God, the life and work of Jesus Christ, the Holy Spirit, resurrection, human sin, salvation, the kingdom of God, creation, and the new heavens and new earth.

Where has your theology been tweaked or corrected as you worked through Hebrews?

How might your understanding of Christian doctrine be lacking without studying Hebrews?

How does the book of Hebrews uniquely contribute to our understanding of God, Jesus Christ, and the Holy Spirit?

Are there specific ways in which Hebrews helps us understand the human condition?

Personal Implications

As you reflect on Hebrews as a whole, and the author's vision of the superiority of Jesus Christ over all things, what implications do you see for your life?

What implications for your life flow from your reflections on the questions already asked in this week's study concerning Gospel Glimpses, Whole-Bible Connections, and Theological Soundings?

How has your faith in the "once-for-all" work of Jesus Christ been deepened?

What have you learned in Hebrews that might lead you to worship God, repent and turn from your sin, and trust more firmly in the gospel of Jesus Christ?

▶ As You Finish Studying Hebrews . . .

We rejoice with you as you finish studying the book of Hebrews! May this study become part of your Christian walk of faith, day by day and week by week throughout all your life. Now we would greatly encourage you to study the Word of God on a week-by-week basis. To continue your study of the Bible, we would encourage you to consider other books in the *Knowing the Bible* series, and to visit www.knowingthebibleseries.org.

Lastly, take a moment to look back through this study. Review the notes that you have written and the things that you have highlighted or underlined. Reflect again on the key themes that the Lord has been teaching you about himself and about his Word. May these things become a treasure for you throughout your life—this we pray, in the name of the Father, and the Son, and the Holy Spirit. Amen.